Artists

VOLUME 4: M-Z

FROM MICHELANGELO TO MAYA LIN

Artists

**Judy Galens and
Mark Swartz**

GALE GROUP
⋆
TM
THOMSON LEARNING

Detroit • New York • San Diego • San Francisco
Boston • New Haven, Conn. • Waterville, Maine
London • Munich

Artists

From Michelangelo to Maya Lin

By Judy Galens and Mark Swartz

Staff

Diane Sawinski, U•X•L Senior Editor
Lawrence W. Baker and Elizabeth Shaw Grunow, U•X•L Contributing Editors
Carol DeKane Nagel, U•X•L Managing Editor
Thomas L. Romig, U•X•L Publisher

Edna Hedblad, Permissions Specialist
Kelly Quin, Senior Image Editor
Pamela Reed, Image Coordinator

Pamela A. E. Galbreath, Senior Art Director

Evi Seoud, Assistant Manager, Composition and Electronic Prepress
Rita Wimberley, Senior Buyer

Synapse Corporation, *indexing*
LM Design, *typesetting*

Cover Artwork: Leonardo da Vinci's *La Gioconda* (*Mona Lisa:* front left) reproduced by permission of Alinari/Art Resource; Andy Warhol portrait (front right) and Henry Moore's *King and Queen* (back left) reproduced by permission of Archive Photos/Express Newspapers.

The Library of Congress has cataloged Volumes 1 and 2 of this title under Library of Congress Control Number 95-186053

ISBN 0-7876-5363-2 (set)
ISBN 0-7876-5364-0 (Volume 3: A-L)
ISBN 0-7876-5365-9 (Volume 4: M-Z)

Copyright © 2002   U•X•L, an imprint of the Gale Group

Printed in the United States of America

10 9 8 7 6 5 4 3 2 1

Contents

UPDATE *indicates update to original entry*

Grant Wood

VOLUME 4: M–Z

Artists by Fields and Media

Bold numerals indicate volume numbers.

Maurice Sendak

Assemblage

Cartoons

Ceramics

Cloth and Textiles

Clothing Design

Collage

Drawing

Environmental Art

Film and Video

Fresco

Furniture Design

Graphic Design

Illustration

Industrial Design

Installation

Interior Design

Jewelry

Landscape Design

Masks

Mobiles

Mosaic

Mural

Painting

Paper Cutouts

Performance Art

Photography

Plastics

Posters

Printmaking (Etching, Engraving, Silkscreening, etc.)

Quilting

Sculpture

Reader's Guide

Betye Saar

A rtists: *From Michelangelo to Maya Lin,* volumes 3 and 4, presents the life stories of 60 sculptors, painters, architects, photographers, illustrators, and designers whose works and ideas have changed the face of art. Concentrating on North American and European artists from the Renaissance to the modern day, *Artists* provides a view of the artists' worlds— their personal experiences and motivations and the social and artistic climates that informed their works—and the impact of their art on society and on future generations of artists. The full-length biographies in volumes 3 and 4 cover artists not included in volumes 1 and 2; ten shorter biographies provide updates on artists featured in past volumes.

Format

The 60 biographies of *Artists* are arranged alphabetically over two volumes. Each entry opens with a portrait of the artist, birth and death information, a short tag indicating the artist's nationality and primary field, and a quote by or about the artist. Accompanying several biographies are boxed sidebar pieces discussing important concepts, movements, and personalities related to the biography, such as neoclassicism, Arts and Crafts, and performance art. Each entry concludes with a list of books, periodicals, and Web sites to explore for more information on that artist. In addition to the artists' portraits, more than 130 photographs illustrate the text.

Each volume begins with a listing of the featured artists by the fields in which they worked and their favored media, a time line showing a work by each artist alongside major historical events, and a glossary of key art terms. The volumes conclude with a general list of books and Web sites for further reading and a cumulative subject index providing easy access to the people, movements, and works mentioned throughout *Artists.*

Dedications

To Brigham and Graham; to my mother, Jane Odell Galens; and in memory of my father, Dr. Gilbert J. Galens

—JG

To Laurel Swartz, Jennie Guilfoyle, and Yoko Ono

—MS

Comments and Suggestions

We welcome your comments on this work as well as your suggestions for individuals to be featured in future editions of *Artists: From Michelangelo to Maya Lin.* Please write: Author, *Artists,* U•X•L, 27500 Drake Road, Farmington Hills, MI 48331-3535; call toll-free: 1-800-877-4253; fax to 248-699-8097; or send e-mail at www.galegroup.com.

Words to Know

Abstract art: An art style in which the subject is not represented in a naturally recognizable manner. Instead of presenting the real appearance of the subject, abstract artists try to express ideas or feelings about the subject through the use of shapes, colors, lines, and other elements. Wassily Kandinsky (1866–1944) is credited with creating the first totally abstract painting. Although abstract art is primarily a modern style, there are elements of abstraction in ancient art, especially in the use of decorative patterns.

Abstract expressionism: A movement of **abstract art** that emerged in New York City during the 1940s and reached its peak in the 1950s. Although abstract expressionists painted in many different styles, they had in common an interest in using paint to show their emotions. They often used thick and sometimes violent brush strokes to create dense textures on large canvases. These artists considered the actions involved in the creation of a painting—including the mistakes made in the

Sandro Botticelli

process—to be as important as the finished work. Some important artists in this highly influential movement were **Jackson Pollock, Mark Rothko** (see entries), and Hans Hofmann.

Academic art: A term used to describe art that obeyed rules set down by the important art academy or school of the day. For example, in nineteenth-century Paris the most successful artists were those who painted in the style approved by the French Academy of Fine Arts, whose standards of beauty derived from ancient Greek and Roman culture. More adventurous artists used this term in a negative manner to describe art they felt was dull and uninventive. See also **Salon.**

Assemblage: A form of sculpture produced when the artist combines objects, often discarded non-art materials found in junkyards. Despite the humble origin of the materials, surprisingly poetic and beautiful assemblages have been produced by **Joseph Cornell** and **Betye Saar** (see entries).

Avante-garde: From a French word meaning "vanguard" or "ahead of its time." When applied to art, avant-garde describes creations that are progressive, innovative, or experimental. Since it challenges established styles, avant-garde work is often controversial.

Baroque: An art style developed in the early 1600s and lasting into the early 1700s. The main characteristic of this style is its sense of unity among the arts of painting, architecture, and sculpture. Reacting against the classical and sometimes severe style of Renaissance art, Baroque artists sought to make their works more lively and emotional. With an emphasis on bright colors, light, and exaggerated forms, many Baroque compositions exhibit a feeling of energy and movement. Baroque style later developed into rococo art. Notable Baroque artists include **Rembrandt van Rijn** (see entry), Peter Paul Rubens, and Diego Velazquez.

Bauhaus: A German design school—begun in 1919 and closed in 1933—founded by the architect Walter Gropius. The Bauhaus was based on the principle that all branches of the arts, from fine arts like sculpture and painting to applied arts like carpentry and graphic design, should be taught together and given equal status (typically the fine arts have been accorded higher status). In a marriage of industrial technology and artistic principles, Bauhaus students sought to create objects for the masses that were both functional and attractive. Classes were taught by expert craftspeople as well as such established fine artists as Wassily Kandinsky and **Paul Klee** (see entry).

Chiaroscuro: The use of contrasting light and dark shades to create a sense of depth, emphasize an emotion, or establish a mood in a painting. Chiaroscuro (kee-AR-uh-SKYOOR-oh) has been used to brilliant effect by many of the world's great painters, notably Leonardo da Vinci, **Michelangelo Caravaggio,** and **Rembrandt van Rijn** (see entries).

Collage: From a French word meaning "gluing" or "pasting." A collage is an artistic composition created when such unrelated materials as cloth, newspaper, wallpaper, string, and wire are combined and pasted on a painted or unpainted surface. See also **photocollage.**

Composition: The way an artist arranges elements on a canvas or in space. Balancing lights and darks or emptiness and filled-in areas, artists "compose" paintings or sculptures according to their sense of how the overall work should appear.

Cubism: An art movement begun in the early 1900s by **Georges Braque** (see entry) and Pablo Picasso. Cubist artists abandoned the desire to render a subject with mood and emotion. Instead, they presented it broken apart into geometric shapes. In this way, they depicted the subject from several points of view at once—an attempt to portray the subject not as the eye sees it but as the mind perceives it. Cubism was one of the most important developments in modern art.

Dadaism: A literary and art movement that began in Switzerland in 1916 and lasted until 1922. Disillusioned by the effects of World War I, Dada artists fought against traditional artistic values, creating art that showed absurd, nonsensical, and violent aspects of life. Some prominent Dada artists were **Marcel Duchamp** (see entry), Man Ray, and Jean Arp.

Engraving: A method of printmaking whereby lines and grooves are cut with a sharp tool into a metal plate (or in some instance a wood block) and then filled with ink. After the surface of the plate is wiped clean, the plate is pressed against absorbent paper, producing an image from the pooled ink. Engravings can be original works by an artist or a way of copying an existing work. See also **etching** and **woodcut.**

Etching: A method of **engraving** that uses a metal plate covered with a layer of acid-resistant wax. The artist draws through the wax with a sharp instrument to reveal portions of the metal plate. Next the plate is dipped in acid, which attacks only the parts where the wax has been scraped away. The plate is covered with ink, then the surface is wiped clean. Afterward, paper is pressed onto the inked plate. The etched portion of the plate, which retains the ink, reveals the artist's drawing. An etching may be printed several times.

Expressionism: A term used to describe art in which the personal feeling of the artist is the most important aspect of the work. Instead of imitating real life, expressionist artists transform it to fit their creative vision. Colors, shapes, and textures are often exaggerated to show emotion. The art of Vincent van Gogh is a well-known example of expressionism. Expressionist styles often have a descriptive word to identify them more specifically, such as **abstract expressionism** or **German expressionism.**

Fauvism: A brief art movement begun by Henri Matisse and other artists in the early twentieth century. These artists were interested in using only pure, strong colors to define structure, generate light, and capture emotion in their paintings. Because the use of color in the resulting works seemed violent and uncontrolled, critics called these artists "fauves," which means "wild beasts" in French.

Feminism: The belief system that seeks social and political equality for women and celebrates the values that women have traditionally upheld, such as creativity and nurturing. Feminism has informed the art of many contemporary women artists, including **Laurie Anderson** and **Cindy Sherman** (see entries).

Folk art: The traditional art of the native inhabitants of a region whose artists have not received any formal artistic training. Many professional artists have used ideas from folk art in their works.

Fresco: From the Italian word for "fresh." A fresco is a wall painting made with pigments, the powdery substances used to make paint. The pigments are mixed with water and applied quickly to a plastered wall while the plaster is still wet. As the plaster dries, the pigment colors are absorbed into the plaster, retaining their bright hues. This technique was perfected during the Italian **Renaissance**, especially by Michelangelo. Fresco painting declined until the modern era, when Diego Rivera sparked a renewed interest in the technique.

German expressionism: A movement active in Germany from before World War I (1914–18) to the early 1930s that emphasized expression of the artist's emotions through the use of harsh, angular lines and bold, disturbing colors. The German expressionists, led in the early 1900s by Ernst Ludwig Kirchner, rebelled against what they felt was the superficial quality of traditional painting styles. They sought to convey their anxiety, fear, and disdain for modern society through their intense and unsettling paintings. The ideas of the German expressionist movement spread to other countries as well, influencing the work of such notable artists as Austria's **Egon Schiele** (see entry) and France's Chaim Soutine.

Gothic: An architectural style seen in buildings made between the twelfth and fifteenth centuries. Gothic elements such as pointed arches and flying buttresses (structural supports that extend beyond the walls of a building) reappeared in modified versions in later centuries.

Impressionism: The most important movement in European art in the late 1800s. Impressionist artists, who were mostly French, explored new theories about light and color. Rather than copying a scene exactly as it looked, they used these theories to capture the "impression" of a scene as they viewed it. They were interested in the ways atmosphere and light changed the way things appeared in nature. Many styles of modern art developed from the ideas of the impressionists. Some important impressionist painters were Claude Monet, **Camille Pissarro** and **Edgar Degas** (see entries). See also **Post-impressionism.**

Lithograph: A print made by drawing with a special grease crayon on a porous stone or on a grained metal plate. When their works. It can also be defined as naive, nonacademic, or **folk art**—art created by people who have not had formal training. Some of Spanish artist Pablo Picasso's works fall into the first category of primitivism, while French artist **Henri Rousseau** (see entry) exemplifies the second definition.

Realism: A mid-nineteenth-century art style whose followers attempted to depict objects and scenes as they existed in real life, without any attempt to make them perfect or ideal. Realist artists focused on scenes of everyday life (most often the "ugly" or commonplace) rather than on biblical or heroic subjects or characters. See also **social realism.**

Renaissance: From a French word meaning "rebirth." The Renaissance was a period of heightened artistic and intellectual activity prompted by a renewed interest in the art and literature of the ancient Greeks and Romans. It began in Italy in the late 1300s and spread through Europe by the 1600s. During the Renaissance, great advances were made in areas such as science and exploration, music, literature, and the visual arts. **Raphael** and **Botticelli** (see entries) were significant Renaissance artists.

Rococo: A decorative style of art and architecture that began in eighteenth-century France and rapidly spread across Europe. A reaction to the heaviness of **Baroque** decoration, the rococo is marked by delicacy and light, and common motifs include shells, scrolls, leaves, and other curving shapes.

Salon des Artistes Français: An annual exhibition, known simply as the Salon, of art works selected by a jury and sponsored by the French Academy of Fine Arts beginning in 1737. It was generally considered a great honor for an artist's work to be exhibited in one of these influential shows. Starting in the mid-nineteenth century, however, when the juries began to favor conservative, established art styles over innovative works, many artists rejected the traditional Salon and opted to display their works in the alternative Salon des Artistes Indépendants. See also **academic art.**

Social realism: A form of **realism** embraced by American artists of the 1920s and 1930s who wanted to use their art to make political and economic statements about society. These artists usually depicted the lives of workers, the poor, and the homeless. Social realism is not defined by one particular artistic style but by subject content. Both **Jacob Lawrence** (see entry) and Diego Rivera were social realists.

Still life: A work of art whose subject is inanimate objects such as flowers, fruits and vegetables, pottery, tableware, and other decorative pieces.

Surrealism: A literary and art movement founded by writer André Breton in Paris in 1924 and practiced internationally into the 1930s. It was grounded in the psychoanalytic theories of Sigmund Freud, particularly those relating to the expression of the imagination as revealed in dreams. Using a range of styles, the surrealists, such as **René Magritte** (see entry) and Salvador Dali, filled their works with fantastic imagery and dream-inspired symbols.

Woodcut: Also known as a woodblock print, a woodcut is a print made from designs cut in relief on wood. The area that is not to be printed as part of the design is carved away. Ink is then rolled on the remaining surface area and paper is applied to the block to produce the desired print. Albrecht Dürer was a master of the woodblock print, the oldest method of printmaking. The designs of Japanese woodblock prints by **Utagawa Hiroshige** (see entry) and others inspired many of the impressionist painters.

Events in Art and History

Norman Rockwell

1302–05   Giotto, The Arena Chapel frescoes

c. 1430–33 Donatello, *David* (bronze)

1434   Jan van Eyck, The Arnolfini Marriage Portrait

1483   Sandro Botticelli, *The Birth of Venus*

1510–11   Raphael, *School of Athens*

1602–04   Michelangelo Caravaggio, *The Deposition*

1642   Rembrandt van Rijn, *The Militia Company of Captain Frans Banning Cocq,* or *The Night Watch*

c. 1658–60 Jan Vermeer, *The Milkmaid*

1212
Children's Crusade begins with 30,000 children departing from France and Germany for Palestine.

mid-1300s
Bubonic plague, the "black death," killed up to half the population of Europe.

1498
On his third voyage across the Atlantic Ocean, Christopher Columbus reaches the coast of South America.

1636
Harvard College is founded in Cambridge, Massachusetts.

1200	1350	1500	1650

1675–1710 Christopher Wren, St. Paul's Cathedral, London, England

1793 William Blake, *The Marriage of Heaven and Hell*

1814 Jean-Auguste-Dominique Ingres, *Grand Odalisque*

1830 Eugène Delacroix, *Liberty Guiding the People*

1833–34 Utagawa Hiroshige, "The Fifty-Three Stations on the Tokaido"

1867 Julia Margaret Cameron, *My Favourite Picture. My Niece Julia*

1871 James Whistler, *Arrangement in Grey and Black: Portrait of the Painter's Mother*

1874 Edgar Degas, *Rehearsal of a Ballet on the Stage*

1880s Louis Comfort Tiffany, Jack-in-the-Pulpit vase

1892–93 John Singer Sargent, *Lady Agnew of Lochnaw*

1893 Edvard Munch, *The Scream*

1895 Frederic Remington, *The Fall of the Cowboy*

1897 Henri Rousseau, *The Sleeping Gypsy*

Camille Pissarro, *Boulevard Montmartre*

1901 Beatrix Potter, *The Tale of Peter Rabbit*

1907–08 Gustav Klimt, *The Kiss*

1909–10 Georges Braque, *Pitcher and Violin*

1911 Egon Schiele, *Pregnant Mother and Death*

1913 Marcel Duchamp, *Bicycle Wheel*

1914 Giorgio de Chirico, *The Song of Love*

1701-14
War of Spanish Succession pits England, the Netherlands, the Holy Roman Empire, and the German states against France.

1799
Discovery of the Rosetta Stone enables Egyptian hieroglyphic writings to be translated by scholars.

1845-51
Potato famine devastates Ireland, causing an estimated one million lives and the immigration of about two million Irish people, primarily to the United States.

1898
Britain acquires the island of Hong Kong from China on a ninety-nine-year lease.

| 1700 | 1750 | 1800 | 1850 | 1900 |

1922 Paul Klee, *Twittering Machine*

1923 Aleksandr Rodchenko, Advertising posters for the state airline Dobrolet

1925 Tina Modotti, *Telephone Wires, Mexico*

1929 René Magritte, *The False Mirror*

1930 Grant Wood, *American Gothic*

1940–41 Joan Miró, The "Constellations" paintings

1941 Jacob Lawrence, "Migration of the Negro" series

1942 Joseph Cornell, *Medici Slot Machine*

1943 Norman Rockwell, "Four Freedoms" series

1944 Francis Bacon, *Three Studies for Figures at the Base of a Crucifixion*

1947–48 Eero Saarinen, Jefferson Westward Expansion Memorial (The Gateway Arch), St. Louis, Missouri

1948 Andrew Wyeth, *Christina's World*

1950 Jackson Pollock, *Lavender Mist: Number 1, 1950*

1950–53 Willem de Kooning, "Woman" series

1955 Jasper Johns, *Flag*

1958 M. C. Escher, *Belvedere*

1962 Roy Lichtenstein, *Blam!*

1963 Maurice Sendak, *Where the Wild Things Are*

1964–67 Mark Rothko, The Rothko Chapel

1966 Yoko Ono, *Ceiling Painting (Yes Painting)*

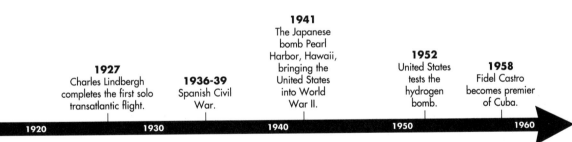

1927 Charles Lindbergh completes the first solo transatlantic flight.

1936-39 Spanish Civil War.

1941 The Japanese bomb Pearl Harbor, Hawaii, bringing the United States into World War II.

1952 United States tests the hydrogen bomb.

1958 Fidel Castro becomes premier of Cuba.

1920   1930   1940   1950   1960

1967	Diane Arbus, *Identical Twins, Roselle, New Jersey*
	Duane Hanson, *Policeman and Rioter*
1972	Betye Saar, *The Liberation of Aunt Jemima*
1979	Cindy Sherman, *Untitled Film Still #48*
1982	Martin Puryear, *Bodark Arc*
	Maya Lin, Vietnam Veterans Memorial, Washington, D.C.
1983	Laurie Anderson, *United States I–IV*
1980s	Keith Haring, *Radiant Baby*
1986	David Hockney, *Pearblossom Hwy. 11–18th April 1986 #2*
1988	Faith Ringgold, *Tar Beach* (quilt)
1989	I. M. Pei, Le Grand Louvre, Paris, France
1991	Lucian Freud, *Head of Leigh Bowery*

1972
United States Supreme Court declares the death penalty to be unconsitutional.

1979
Margaret Thatcher becomes the first female prime minister of Britian.

1986
The space shuttle *Challenger* explodes, killing all seven aboard.

1997
China regains control of Hong Kong.

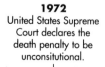

1970　　　1980　　　1990　　　2000

Artists

René Magritte

Born November 21, 1898
Lessines, Belgium

Died August 15, 1967
Brussels, Belgium

Belgian painter

W hile their unusual titles may escape the viewer's memory, René Magritte's bizarre and mysterious paintings make a deep impression. Magritte is usually associated with the surrealists, a group of artists and writers centered in Paris, France, in the 1920s and 1930s. The surrealists sought to merge the real world with a world of fantasy, resulting in startling, dreamlike works. Magritte painted in an ultra-realistic, almost photographic style, but by combining elements that do not ordinarily belong together, he fashioned a world that departed from reality. He felt that the everyday world is mysterious and frequently nonsensical, and his paintings are filled with common objects—like hats, eggs, loaves of bread, and windows—put together in uncommon ways to reflect that belief. In addition to having an enormous impact on modern fine art, Magritte's works also profoundly affected commercial art: images from Magritte's paintings have been used to advertise everything from televisions to typewriters to cosmetics.

"My painting is visible images which conceal nothing; they evoke mystery . . ."

▲ *René Magritte.*
Reproduced by permission of Archive Photos.

An early tragedy

The oldest of three sons born to Léopold and Régina Magritte, René François Ghislain Magritte (pronounced muh-GREET) spent much of his childhood in the Belgian city of Châtelet, in a house near the River Sambre. When he was fourteen, Magritte's mother committed suicide by drowning herself in the Sambre. Magritte later told a biographer that when his mother's body was found, her nightgown had risen up to cover her face. In truth, the young Magritte probably did not see his mother's body as it was retrieved from the river. The image of a covered face, though most likely created in his imagination rather than existing as a memory, was a powerful one for Magritte. Faces draped with cloth, as well as dark and forbidding depictions of water, appear in many of his paintings.

Magritte began drawing and painting at the age of twelve, attending local art classes. He continued to develop his skills throughout his teen years, neglecting other school subjects in favor of art. In 1916, Magritte enrolled in the Académie Royale des Beaux-Arts, the school of fine arts located in Brussels, Belgium. He studied there for a few years, learning the basics of art education and meeting a number of young artists and poets with whom he discussed the exciting new developments emerging in modern art. Magritte served in the army in 1920–21, after which he found work designing wallpaper. He later worked as a commercial artist, creating posters and designs for advertising. In 1922, he married Georgette Berger, a woman he had first met when he was fifteen years old and who remained his wife until his death in 1967.

Throughout the early 1920s, Magritte was involved in experimental art, periodicals, and theater. His paintings from this period reflect the influence of cubism, a significant early twentieth-century movement that presented its subjects as groupings of geometric shapes. In 1922 or 1923, Magritte encountered a reproduction of the painting *The Song of Love,* by Italian artist **Giorgio de Chirico** (1888–1978; see entry in volume 3). An odd juxtaposition of such elements as a ball, a rubber glove, and the head of an ancient statue, this painting moved

Magritte and opened up a whole new world for him. He called it "triumphant poetry" that challenges "the stereotyped effect of traditional painting." In the mid-1920s, Magritte became involved with the Belgian surrealists. Aiming to question reality and to stir up bourgeois (pronounced BOORZH-wah), or middle class, ideas of what art should be, the surrealists created strange and unusual works of art. Magritte's first solo exhibition, in Brussels in 1927, was not a critical success. A few months later, Magritte and his wife moved to Paris, the center of the surrealist movement and a hotbed of intellectual and artistic activity.

After moving to Paris, Magritte became acquainted with several writers and artists of the surrealist movement, including French poets André Breton (1896–1966) and Paul Éluard (1895–1952). Throughout the three years he spent in Paris, Magritte sharpened his technical skills, experimented with different methods and effects, and became increasingly involved with the surrealists. In the end, however, while always maintaining ties with them, Magritte discovered significant differences between himself and the French surrealists. He felt they were too rigid in their artistic requirements, and their works tended to be more violent and shocking than his. In 1930, the Magrittes returned home to Belgium. Magritte felt more aligned with Belgian surrealists, and he and his wife had a large circle of friends including artists, writers, and intellectuals. Magritte enjoyed his domestic routine and disliked travel; consequently, except for occasional travel, he stayed in Belgium for the rest of his life.

Pipes and bowler hats

By the time he returned to Belgium, Magritte had established the style with which he is usually identified: precise, realistically painted figures and common objects assembled in startling and unusual ways. Apart from a period of experimentation in the 1940s, Magritte's style did not deviate dramatically for the rest of his life. What did change was the subject matter: Magritte painted a vast array of objects, choosing a theme that interested him and returning to it again and again. The pictorial element for which Magritte is perhaps most famous is that of a man in a business suit and a bowler, a dome-shaped hat with a narrow brim. To many people, this style of dress represented the prim and proper bourgeoisie, a class of people that Magritte both belonged to and wished to challenge with his startling images. *Golconda,* one of Magritte's most recognizable pictures, shows dozens of men dressed in suits and bowler hats, floating through the sky in front of an apartment building.

People frequently questioned Magritte about the meaning of his paintings, wondering what the strange images could symbolize. Annoyed by such questions, Magritte wanted his works to be taken at face value, to be appreciated for the thoughts and feelings they evoke, not for any hidden meaning. He wrote: "To equate my painting with symbolism, conscious or unconscious, is to ignore its true nature. . . . People who look for symbolic meanings fail to grasp the inherent poetry and mystery of the image." Intent on jolting viewers' expectations, Magritte used optical illusion and his keen imagination to present an alternative reality. In *Time Transfixed,* what appears to be a fully operational steam engine emerges from the wall of a fireplace in a pleasant, middle-class living room. In *The Listening-Room,* a giant green apple fills an entire room and even seems to go beyond the canvas, giving the viewer a sense of claustrophobia. A number of paintings, several of which were called *The Human Condition,* show a canvas propped on an easel in front of a window. The scene painted on the canvas blends in with the landscape viewed through the window. Part of the scene outside is blocked by the painting on the inside of the room, leaving the viewer to wonder about what is hidden behind the canvas.

A devoted and knowledgeable reader of literature and poetry, Magritte frequently incorporated words into his paintings. He explored the meaning, or more often meaninglessness, of words, giving an absurd treatment to the ability of words to describe a picture: many of his paintings show familiar objects with labels beneath them, though often those labels do not correspond at all to the image. In the 1927 painting *The Interpretation of Dreams,* for example, Magritte has divided the canvas into four sections, with an object in each. A leaf is labeled *la table,* or "the table," while a knife is labeled

Le Domaine. *Painting by René Magritte.*
Reproduced by permission of Archive Photos.

l'oiseau, or "the bird." (In many instances, Magritte painted a series of similar works and gave them all the same title; several of his paintings are titled *The Interpretation of Dreams,* which is also the title of a famous book by Austrian psychoanalyst Sigmund Freud [1856–1939].) One of his best-known works, called *The Treachery of Images,* is a clearly and realistically drawn picture of a pipe. Beneath the pipe is the phrase

Ceci n'est pas une pipe, which translates to "this is not a pipe." With this painting, Magritte seems to suggest that there is little connection between an image and the word used to describe it, or between a real object and a drawing of that object. The titles of his paintings, which usually seem to have no relation to the paintings themselves, further demonstrate Magritte's playful approach to the relationship between word and image.

A subject that Magritte painted many times, and in many different ways, is the nude female body. One of his most famous works, called *The Rape,* is a sort of visual joke depicting a face, the parts of which double as a naked woman's torso. Whether seen as amusing or disturbing, or both, this painting is not soon forgotten by the viewer. A number of Magritte's paintings of the female body, including *The Importance of Marvels* and *Megalomania,* show the body divided into sections that nest within each other. This theme was repeated in a large bronze sculpture, also called *Megalomania,* that Magritte designed in the last year of his life. In *Discovery,* painted in 1927, Magritte combines his interest in painting the female nude with an exploration of metamorphosis, or transformation, a concept he addressed in numerous paintings. Parts of the woman's flesh in *Discovery* have transformed into a highly grained wood, which also resembles the striped fur of a jungle animal. Magritte felt that creating this effect was a significant development in his painting. He wrote to his friend and fellow surrealist Paul Nougé: "By this means I produce pictures in which the eye must 'think' in a completely different way."

A period of stylistic departure

In the late 1930s, as World War II (1939–45) took hold, Magritte attempted to rouse himself from a depressed state by taking an entirely new approach to his art. He felt that his work needed refreshing, and he also felt an obligation to help people forget about the devastation of war. Thus began a period of radical departure for Magritte that lasted throughout the 1940s. In the first part of that decade, Magritte experimented with brightly colored, pleasant paintings done in the style of the impressionists. Impressionism, developed in late nineteenth-century France, explored different ways of capturing the light and color of nature. The light, cheerful colors, soft brush strokes, and imprecise lines of Magritte's impressionist works proved dramatically different from the cool tones and clean lines of his earlier works. At the end of the 1940s, he veered in yet another direction, creating works that resembled the style of the fauves, a French word that means "wild beasts." The fauves, led by Henri Matisse (1869–1954; see entry in volume 2) in the early twentieth century, used a rough style of thick lines and vivid colors in their paintings. Many of Magritte's fauve paintings were created expressly for an exhibition to be held in Paris in 1948, and his goal was to shock the Parisians with his bold and even cartoonish new style. His experiment worked, perhaps too well. The critics, many of whom included his old surrealist friends, were surprised and disappointed with Magritte's new direction, and he soon abandoned his exploration into new styles.

Masterworks	
1927	*Discovery*
1929	*The False Mirror*
	The Treachery of Images
1933	*Elective Affinities*
	The Human Condition
1934	*The Rape*
1938	*Time Transfixed*
1953	*Golconda*
1952	*The Listening-Room*
	Personal Values

Magritte settled back into his former routines, and in the 1950s he began to achieve major commercial success and international recognition. His paintings were selling well and museums in the United States and throughout Europe displayed his works. A major retrospective at New York's Museum of Modern Art in 1965 signaled Magritte's status as a prominent modern artist. While financial success must have eased some of Magritte's burden, friends speculated that with the success came some degree of guilt—a feeling that, in gaining widespread acceptance, he had abandoned his true artistic principles. In any case, illness and extreme fatigue decreased Magritte's interest in new paintings in his final years. His last artistic effort involved designing several sculptures to be based on his paintings; these sculptures were cast in bronze after his death in August 1967. While Magritte's paintings have made their way into the mainstream, particularly in terms of their presence in the world of advertising, they still possess the ability to startle and haunt the viewer. In the years since his death, Magritte has been recognized the world over as an influential force in twentieth-century art.

For More Information

Books and Periodicals

Alden, Todd. *The Essential René Magritte.* Kansas City, MO: Andrews McMeel Publishing, 1999.

Gardner, James. "Homeboys of the Bourgeoisie." *National Review* 44 (November 2, 1992): p. 64.

Hammacher, Abraham Marie. *René Magritte.* Translated by James Brockway. New York: Abradale Press, 1995.

Schiff, Bennett. "The Artist Who Was Master of the Double Take." *Smithsonian* 23 (September 1992): p. 48.

Sylvester, David. *Magritte.* Antwerp, Belgium: Mercatorfonds, 1992.

Updike, John. "It's the Surreal Thing!" *Los Angeles Magazine* 41 (September 1996): p. 80.

Web Sites

"An Extraordinary Universe: Magritte's Work." *The Montreal Museum of Fine Arts.* [Online] Available http://www.mbam.qc.ca/expopassees/a-magritte.html (last accessed on July 2, 2001).

The Magritte Site. [Online] Available http://www.magritte.com/ (last accessed on July 2, 2001).

"René Magritte." *Mark Harden's Artchive.* [Online] Available http://www.artchive.com/artchive/M/magritte.html (last accessed on July 2, 2001).

Joan Miró

Born April 20, 1893
Barcelona, Spain
Died December 25, 1983
Palma, Spain

Painter and sculptor

oan Miró's long and varied art career spanned most of the developments and revolutions in modern art. His works show a consistently playful attitude and willingness to experiment, whether it emerges in portraits, landscapes, or completely abstract forms. He did not invent the practice of abstraction, in which colors and lines appear on the canvas without obviously representing something in the visible world, but he accomplished much within this challenging arena. Above all, Miró's art displays his talent for inventing images to correspond with poetry, music, and dreams that touched him. He was not as influential or radical as his friend and fellow Spaniard Pablo Picasso (1881–1973; see entry in volume 2), but Miró contributed significantly to the acceptance of modern art in Europe and America.

Although no single artwork captures the range of Miró's accomplishment, a close look at a painting from the 1930s, *Hirondelle—Amour* turns up many of the qualities that distin-

"I wasn't interested in fighting unless I could win the prize."

▲ **Joan Miró.** © *Isabel Steva Hernandez (Colita). Reproduced by permission of the Corbis Corporation.*

guish his style. The French word *hirondelle* means "swallow," which is a type of bird, and *amour* means "love." The painting has numerous recognizable parts, including a shadowy head, a hand, and a bird perched on what looks to be a foot, along with the words that make up the title. The meaning that connects these parts may not be clear, but a spirit of celebration is apparent as they stand together against a richly colored blue background that may or may not represent the sky. Miró's approach is complex enough to appeal to critics and historians, yet simple enough for a child to understand.

Grows up in Spain

Joan Miró (pronounced mee-ROW) Ferrà was born in Barcelona, which is in the Catalan region of Spain. The Catalan people have their own language and a fierce regional pride. The artist's father was a watchmaker, and his mother took care of their four children, of which Joan was the eldest. He embarked on a brief career in business before suffering a nervous breakdown. His family bought a house in the town of Montroig, where he recuperated before starting artistic training under a teacher named Francesc Galí at the Escola d'Art (School of Art) in Barcelona. He worked with Galí from 1912 to 1915, and during this time he first met E. C. Ricart (1893–1960), an artist who would be his closest friend for many years.

Spain was neutral during World War I (1914–18), but the army was prepared to participate. In 1915, Miró was drafted into military service, but when off duty he pursued his art. Among his first mature works is *Portrait of E. C. Ricart* (1917), which shows his friend in a black-and-white striped shirt. A painter's palette is seen floating in the air, and behind the figure is a Japanese print, which Miró pasted directly onto the canvas. Adding bits of work not created by the artist, such as wallpaper or newspaper, was a method commonly employed by the cubists, a loose affiliation of artists in Paris that included **Georges Braque** (1882–1963; see entry in volume 3), Picasso, and another Spaniard, Juan Gris (1887–1927). Starting around 1905, the cubists had sought new ways of making portraits, still-lifes, and landscapes, and their innovations took several years to win over the artistic community, and even then it was only the most adventurous among them.

Moves to Paris

In 1917, Miró attended an exhibition of French art, and this perhaps marked the beginning of his desire to relocate to what was at the time the undisputed center of the art world. A letter he wrote to Ricart in November of 1918 includes the word "Paris" three times in capital letters. The move was a financial strain, however, and he and his friend did not arrive until February of 1920. They immediately gained an introduction to Picasso, who was a major influence on the artists. Picasso was twelve years older and had already found international acclaim while nurturing his Spanish roots. Miró's *Horse, Pipe, and Red Flower*, painted that summer, shows the unmistakable influence of Picasso in its choice of subject matter, but the younger artist was much freer with bright colors. The toy horse, for example, is decorated with orange and yellow balls.

The friendship with Ricart came under pressure as Miró found new associates, including American writer Ernest Hemingway (1899–1961), who bought Miró's *The Farm* as an engagement present in 1925, the same year Hemingway published his first collection of stories, *In Our Time.* This painting, as with many created during this time, has the strange yet familiar feeling of a dream, which might have something to do with the artist's growing association with the painters and poets of the newest movement to hit Paris, surrealism. This group looked to dreams for inspiration, and to what Austrian psychoanalyst Sigmund Freud (1856–1939) termed "the unconscious," a part of everyone's identity that generally remains hidden. For many, following the unconscious led to disturbing imagery of a sexual or violent nature.

By 1924, Miró had to some extent shifted his admiration away from Picasso and toward **Paul Klee** (pronounced CLAY; 1879–1940; see entry in volume 3), a Swiss artist whose work was related but not directly tied to surrealism. Like the surrealists,

"The immense moral, intuitive, and physical concentration Miró imposed on himself in making these little paintings sparked what is arguably the most brilliant expression of his inner vision."

Carolyn Lanchner, referring to the "Constellations" series

Klee employed dreamlike imagery, but unlike them, Klee managed to preserve the innocence in his paintings and drawings. It is likely that Klee's works reminded Miró of the fantastical buildings and churches created by Antonio Gaudí (1852–1926; see entry in volume 1) in his hometown of Barcelona.

Meanwhile, Miró shuttled back and forth between Paris, Barcelona, and Montroig, where he painted *The Policeman* (1925), one of many works that show Klee's influence. The painting features a man and a horse, but the horse in this picture is drastically different from the one in *Horse, Pipe, and Red Flower.* In the earlier work, the animal is quite easily identifiable, but here it is a slender white blob, its identity given away by three strokes of paint that suggest a mane. The policeman beside it is formed from two white blobs, one for the head and one for the body. He has an absurdly long mustache and a single, oversized red hand. As the years went on, Miró grew disenchanted with the surrealists, not so much because of their artistic principles but for political reasons; many of the group's leaders were staunch socialists. Furthermore, his recurrent trips to Spain distanced him from the activities of the group's leaders. In the fall of 1929, he married Pilar Juncosa, the daughter of family friends, and they had a daughter the following summer. Around this time, the artist began experimenting with sculpture, constructing objects from wood and other materials, which he sometimes painted.

Career and life change in 1936

The Museum of Modern Art in New York held an exhibition in the spring of 1936 titled "Cubism and Abstract Art." Miró's presence in the show was a sign that he was achieving international recognition, and numerous gallery and museum shows in New York followed. That summer, civil war broke out in Spain, and until 1940 the artist spent more time in Paris, although he was deeply concerned about the fate of his homeland and of his mother, who still lived there. It is possible to detect the fear and violence in his work during these years. Although there is no obvious political imagery or reference to the war in them, a series of paintings simply titled *Head*

express these emotions through wide-open eyes and twisted mouths. In a letter to art dealer Pierre Matisse, Miró wrote, "The situation in Spain is very agonizing, but far from being desperate we have the firm hope that some event will take

place to tip the balance in our favor. . . . Luckily, I have managed to keep my working enthusiasm and discipline."

The Spanish Civil War (1936–39) overlapped with the start of World War II (1939–45), and soon Miró had to leave the German-occupied Paris for a quiet town called Varengeville. Retreating from the horrible events sweeping across Europe, he developed a new style that reflected the calm after which he sought. In 1940, he launched "Constellations," a series of works done in gouache, a painting technique similar to watercolor. These paintings are among his most famous and important works. They involve bright reds, greens, and blues formed into shapes and designs inspired by the night sky and transformed by the artist's imagination into women, birds, and snails, as well as unrecognizable abstractions. Black dots of varying sizes suggest musical notes. He gave many of the "Constellations" paintings lengthy, mysterious titles such as *On the 13th, the Ladder Brushed the Firmament* and *Woman with Blond Armpit Combing Her Hair by the Light of the Stars.*

Enlarges his international reputation

Miró was fifty-two years old when World War II ended, and he was determined to continue developing as an artist. He was motivated by the example of Pablo Picasso, who continued to work in all mediums well into old age. He executed a number of small sculptures in ceramic, bronze, and stone, usually creating human figures that were distorted in some way, such as with huge eyes or feet.

As a painter, Miró was not through yet. In 1946, he was commissioned to execute a mural in a hotel in Cincinnati, Ohio. In the early 1960s, he drastically simplified his technique, covering canvases in a single color in works such as *Blue III* and *Mural Painting III*. The painter would add one or two lines or spots to these large fields of blue or red, managing to convey deep emotions with the simplest means possible. By this time, the breakthroughs of Miró, Klee, and other painters had become acceptable practices beyond Paris, especially in New York, where a new generation of painters would go even further. Artists such as Arshile Gorky (1905–1948), Robert Motherwell (1915–1991), and **Mark Rothko** (1903–1970; see entry in volume 4) all profited from Miró's monochromatic, or single-color, paintings.

In 1976, the Joan Miró Foundation opened in Barcelona. This institution was created for the preservation and celebration of the artist's work. As his fame continued to spread, more commissions came his way, including one for a large public sculpture in Chicago, called *Miss Chicago* (1981). Miró died on Christmas Day, 1983, about six months after the Museum of Modern Art held an exhibition titled "Joan Miró: A Ninetieth-Birthday Tribute."

Masterworks	
1917	*Portrait of E. C. Ricart*
1920	*Horse, Pipe, and Red Flower*
1921–22	*The Farm*
1925	*The Policeman*
1933–34	*Hirondelle—Amour*
1940–41	The "Constellations" paintings
1981	*Miss Chicago*

For more information

Books

Blanquet, Claire-Helene. *Miró: Earth and Sky.* Broomall, PA: Chelsea House, 1994.

Danto, Arthur C. *Encounters & Reflections: Art in the Historical Present.* Berkeley: University of California Press, 1997.

Lanchner, Carolyn. *Joan Miró.* New York: The Museum of Modern Art, 1993.

Rowell, Margit. *Joan Miró: Selected Writings and Interviews.* New York: Da Capo Press, 1992.

Web Sites

"Joan Miró." *Mark Harden's Artchive.* [Online]

Available http://www.artchive.com/artchive/M/miro.html (last accessed on July 2, 2001).

Tina Modotti

Born August 17, 1896
Udine, Italy

Died January 5, 1942
Mexico City, Mexico

Italian photographer

I n *Tina Modotti: Photographs,* Sarah M. Lowe describes Modotti as "the best-known unknown photographer of the twentieth century." Modotti's status as a significant but unfamiliar photographer may be due in part to the fact that most of her creative output occurred over a brief period, while she was living in Mexico between 1923 and 1930. Her lack of recognition as a photographer can also be explained by the notion that scholars have paid more attention to her fascinating and controversial life—filled with world travel, radical politics, and high-profile romances—than to her artistic work. Modotti reinvented herself many times throughout her life, working as an actress in San Francisco and Hollywood, modeling for famous photographers, becoming a photographer herself in Mexico, and eventually abandoning art for a life as a Communist revolutionary.

Some biographers have suggested that Modotti thrived on mystery and playacting, and as a result the details of her life seem rather vague and are cause for endless speculation.

"Art cannot exist without life I admit but . . . in my case life is always struggling to predominate and art naturally suffers."

In a letter to Edward Weston, 1925

Although it cannot be completely separated from her turbulent life, Modotti's photography can be evaluated on its own for its artistic merit and social conscience. Trained by American photographer Edward Weston (1886–1958; see box), Modotti initially battled the impression that she was no more than his talented student and imitator, but recent scholarly evaluations have assessed her work as important in its own right. Whether photographing flowers, telephone wires, or the poverty-stricken Mexican natives with whom she identified so strongly, Modotti approached her subjects with a keen eye and a sensitive heart.

Modotti's many lives

Assunta Adelaide Luigia Modotti (called Tina from Assuntina, a modification of her first name) was born in Udine, a town in northern Italy, to Assunta and Guiseppe Modotti. The working-class Modotti family moved to Austria in 1898 in the hopes of finding better jobs. They lived there for seven years, earning enough to survive but suffering from the harsh discrimination many Austrians directed at immigrants. According to her family, this experience may have been the source of Modotti's social activism. The family returned to Udine in 1905, and that same year Modotti's father left for the United States. Over the next several years, Modotti attended school and worked in a factory to help support her family. She may have learned something about photography from her uncle, Pietro Modotti, who was a successful portrait photographer and instructor in Udine. In 1913, Modotti left Italy to join her father in San Francisco.

According to family accounts, Modotti worked as a seamstress in the garment industry when she first arrived in San Francisco. She later got involved in the vibrant theater scene among the city's community of Italian immigrants. She may have started out sewing costumes, but by 1917 she was onstage, winning favorable reviews and local fame. In 1915, she met Roubaix de l'Abrie Richey (1890–1922), an artist and poet known as "Robo" who shared Modotti's knack for adopting a mysterious and interesting persona, or role. Born Ruby Richey on a farm in Oregon, Robo reinvented himself as an elegant, city-bred Frenchman. Likewise, Modotti was beginning to shed her past as an uneducated working-class girl, acquiring a sophistication and cultural education that would suit her artistic lifestyle. She and Richey married in 1918, the same year they moved to Hollywood so Modotti could become a film actress. She earned a living modeling for artists and photographers, and she did land several film roles, including a major part in the 1920 silent film *The Tiger's Coat.*

Modotti and Richey became the center of a social circle that included artists, musicians, and writers, some of whom were involved in left-wing politics. Richey occasionally provided illustrations for the radical *Gale's International Journal for Revolutionary Communism,* a magazine that occasionally reported on the struggles of laborers and the establishment of the Mexican Communist Party in Mexico. (Communism is an economic and political system in which all property is owned by the state, and wealth is distributed among the citizens according to their need.) In 1921, Modotti met photographer Edward Weston, who had begun to establish himself as an important advocate of photographic realism. Many of his peers created pictures in imitation of paintings, shooting with a soft focus and manipulating images in a darkroom to achieve a desired effect. Weston had come to prefer a highly detailed, starkly realistic style. Modotti began modeling for him, and they soon became lovers. Still married to Richey, Modotti (and Weston as well) planned to follow her husband to Mexico after he moved there late in 1921. A few months later, before Modotti arrived, Richey died of smallpox. In spite of her deepening involvement with Weston, Modotti was deeply grieved by Robo's death, and her mourning intensified a few weeks later when her father died. More than a year later, in 1923, Modotti finally made the move to Mexico, with Weston at her side.

Life in Mexico

Mexico in the 1920s was home to a vibrant artistic community and an active left-wing political movement, both of which appealed enormously to Modotti. She had already begun to learn about the business of professional photography from Weston, and she was determined to become a photographer her-

Edward Weston

One of the most important photographers of the twentieth century, Edward Weston sought to "present with utmost exactness" the objects, bodies, and landscapes he photographed. Born in Highland Park, Illinois, Weston spent most of his adult life in California. He became a well-known portrait photographer, operating his own studio in Tropico (now Glendale), California, from 1911 to 1922. In those early years as a photographer, Weston was a pictorialist, meaning that he manipulated the lighting, focus, and development of his prints to make them look like impressionistic paintings. Attending an exhibition of modern art in 1915, however, set Weston on a different creative path. He eventually turned 180 degrees from his initial style to create works that were starkly realistic—what he described in his book *America and Photography* (1929) as "a photography free from technical tricks and incoherent emotionalism."

In 1923, Weston left his wife and children in California and moved to Mexico with his lover, Tina Modotti. While in Mexico, in addition to starting Modotti on an independent and successful career as a photographer, Weston befriended key figures in Mexico's modern art world, including Diego Rivera and David Siqueiros (1896–1974). With their encouragement, he continued to develop his straightforward, realistic approach. Weston returned to California in 1926 and spent the next two decades developing a body of work that would influence generations of photographers.

Weston is best known for his images of the nude human body, California landscapes, and close-up shots of ordinary objects like green peppers and seashells. By isolating such objects (in works like

self. In exchange for being his darkroom assistant and helping to run his studio, Modotti arranged for Weston to teach her how to take photographs. Quickly adapting both to life in Mexico and to her newfound artistic skills, Modotti had, within her first year there, established friendships with numerous important artists, notably Diego Rivera (1886–1957; see entry in volume 2), and taken her first significant photographs. Reflecting her fascination with geometric shapes and clean lines, Modotti's early works include photographs of telephone wires, staircases, and centuries-old Mexican buildings. She also took several still-life pictures of plants and flowers, exploring their unusual shapes and poetic potential rather than simply capturing their

Shells and *Pepper No. 30*) and capturing them at close range and in sharp detail, Weston revealed the graceful, sculptural qualities in everyday things. His images of rocky coasts, trees, and sand dunes at Point Lobos, California, indicate his love of nature and his conviction that such images need not be altered by a photographer's "tricks" to show the region's stark beauty.

Weston's dedication to realism meant that he refrained from making even slight alterations when developing his images. He used a large-format camera that produced large negatives—that way he could develop a photograph without enlarging it, retaining as much detail as possible. (The more a print is enlarged, the less sharp the details are.) He did not take advantage of any darkroom techniques to make an image lighter or darker, bigger or smaller. The resulting photograph was as close as

Edward Weston. Photograph by John Springer. Reproduced by permission of the Corbis Corporation.

possible to the view he saw through his camera's lens. Weston strictly adhered to realist principles and yet created images that emphasized the poetic and exotic qualities of otherwise ordinary things.

beauty. In her 1924 print *Roses,* for example, Modotti produced a close-up image of four wilted blossoms that are visually interesting as well as touching reminders that a rose's beauty is short-lived. *Flor de Manita* (1925) depicts a bizarre plant with a flower that resembles, in author Sarah Lowe's words, a "desperate, wretched grasping hand."

A large number of Modotti's photographs, including both formal studio works and pictures taken in the streets of Mexico City, feature people. Operating out of Weston's studio, Modotti took numerous portraits of friends and associates. Her sensitive, insightful approach is evident in her subjects' relaxed

accused of being involved in his murder, but she was soon cleared of all charges. Her anti-government activities had made her unpopular with Mexico's leaders, and when an assassination attempt was made on Mexico's new president, Pascual Ortiz Rubio, in early 1930, Modotti was one of many political agitators who were arrested for the crime. Two weeks later, she was forced to leave Mexico.

Modotti ended up in Berlin, Germany, where she lived for a few months, taking some pictures and continuing to fight for the Communist cause. She left Berlin for the Soviet Union in October 1930, embarking on a decade of political missions performed throughout Europe for the Communist party. For the remainder of her life, she was involved with Vittorio Vidali, an Italian who many historians believe worked as a spy for Joseph Stalin (1879–1953), the brutally repressive leader of the Soviet Union. After working on behalf of the losing side in the Spanish Civil War (1936–39), Modotti fled Europe for the United States. She was refused entry by suspicious immigration officials and sent to the country she had been forced out of nearly ten years earlier: Mexico. She lived in Mexico for the remaining few years of her life, first under an assumed name, and later under her own name. While there are no known photographs taken by her during this period, her reputation based on her earlier works continued to grow. On January 5, 1942, after dining in a restaurant, Modotti got in a taxi to go home. At some point during that ride, according to official records, she suffered congestive heart failure and died. Some have suggested that the diagnosis may have been a false one, designed to cover up a murder, but no conclusive evidence has been discovered to support that theory. For those who believe she was murdered, however, Tina Modotti's death became as intriguing and mysterious as her life.

For More Information

Books

Cacucci, Pino. *Tina Modotti: A Life.* Translated by Patricia J. Duncan. New York: St. Martin's Press, 1999.

Hooks, Margaret. *Tina Modotti.* New York: Aperture, 1999.

Lowe, Sarah M. *Tina Modotti: Photographs.* New York: Harry N. Abrams, Inc., 1995.

Web Sites

Tina Modotti. [Online] Available http://www.modotti.com/ (last accessed on July 2, 2001).

"Tina Modotti." *Masters of Photography.* [Online] Available http://www.masters-of-photography.com/M/modotti/ modotti.html (last accessed on July 2, 2001).

Edvard Munch

Born December 12, 1863
Löten, Norway

Died January 23, 1944
Ekely, Norway

**Norwegian painter and
graphic artist**

"My task is the study of the soul, that is to say the study of my own self. . . . In my art I have sought to explain my life and its meaning."

When Edvard Munch came of age as an artist, the primary aim of the artistic establishment in Norway was to render scenes of the outside world as faithfully and as objectively as possible. For Munch, however, art was a way to express the pleasure and pain of the inner life. His paintings are deeply personal, revealing his own psychological scars as well as reflecting the anguish and tension of society. He sought to evoke deep and sometimes disturbing feelings in his audience, believing that the expression of such feelings is art's true purpose. That belief, as well as Munch's particular style, had a major impact on the development of German expressionism at the turn of the century. Munch created a body of work that is vast and significant, but he is most readily identified with one work: the 1893 painting *The Scream*. One of the most recognizable artworks ever produced, *The Scream* has become a symbol of the anxiety and psychological terrors of modern life.

A tragic youth

As a close look at his paintings might suggest, Edvard Munch's childhood was lonely and tragic. His mother, Laura, died of tuberculosis when Munch was just five years old. After her death, Munch's father, Christian, became depressed and extremely religious. Caught up in grief and religious fervor, Christian occasionally behaved erratically and harshly toward his children. When Munch was fourteen years old, his sister Sophie, who was one year older, died of the same disease that had taken his mother. Munch expressed the trauma of witnessing his sister's illness repeatedly in his paintings. He spent much of his youth battling sickness and a weak constitution. "Illness, insanity and death," Munch said, "were the black angels that kept watch over my cradle and accompanied me all my life."

After his mother died, Munch and his siblings were cared for by their mother's sister. A landscape painter, she noticed Munch's gift for drawing, and she bought him art supplies and encouraged his development. As a young man, Munch expressed the desire to become an artist, but his father initially opposed the idea, objecting to what he felt was a lifestyle of loose morals and dim financial prospects. Eventually he gave his son approval, and in the early 1880s Munch began studying and practicing art full time. Even in some of his earliest works, as in a portrait of his sister Inger from 1884, Munch displayed the skills of a mature painter.

Initially Munch associated with the art community in the major Norwegian city of Christiania (now Oslo), studying under highly regarded Norwegian painter Christian Krohg (1852–1925). Krohg was a member of a group of painters called the Christiania Bohème. These artists were dedicated to a bohemian, or unconventional, lifestyle, but they painted in the traditional academic style of painting prevalent in Europe at the time. Extended trips to Paris in 1885 and again in 1889 exposed Munch to the departure from that style in the work of the impressionists and synthetists. The impressionists, led by such painters as Edouard Manet (1832–1883; see entry in volume 2) and Claude Monet (1840–1926; see entry in volume 2), sought to break away from the rigors of traditional painting, creating a new way to capture the fleeting moments of everyday life. Synthetism, made famous by French artist Paul Gauguin (1848–1903; see entry in volume 1), advocated the use of strong, curving lines, a simplified form, and bold, unnatural colors to convey meaning. Eventually, Munch forged his own unique style. He borrowed elements from various traditions, but his works were ultimately defined by his own inner experience.

Early exhibits spark controversy

In 1886, Munch created a stir at a Norwegian exhibition with his painting *The Sick Child*. Arising from his experience with the deaths of his sister and mother, this painting is a raw display of emotion. The ailing girl lies in her bed, looking hopefully out the window. Her mother sits beside the bed, her head bowed in despair. Critics responded angrily to this painting, objecting to its unfinished quality and the scratches made in the surface by the back of the painter's brush. Describing such unconventional works, one Norwegian critic complained that Munch painted "without regard to established laws and forms and often associated with a tendency to fantasy." Munch, however, felt that *The Sick Child* was "a breakthrough in my art. Most of my later works," he wrote, "owe their existence to this picture."

Munch lived in Paris and in Berlin, Germany, for several years in the 1890s, and it was in Berlin in the early part of the decade that his fame began to spread across Europe. In 1892, he displayed several works at an exhibition put on by the Association of Berlin Artists. Munch's unusual paintings shocked the Berlin public, and the resulting outcry led the Association's more conservative members to close the show. What could have been a setback actually resulted in two positive developments. The incident gave Munch immediate fame, enabling him to set up later exhibitions and sell his paintings. Additionally, the younger members of the Association broke off from the group to establish the Neue Berlin Sezession (New Berlin Secession) movement, which later led to the emergence of German expressionism. An extremely important movement in

modern art, expressionism held that the painter's emotional and psychological experiences were more important than adhering to any particular style or convention. Rather than capture a moment in history or everyday life, the expressionists sought to reveal a state of mind and frequently used unnatural, exaggerated lines and colors to communicate meaning and emotion.

Death in the Sickroom (1892). Painting by Edvard Munch. Scala/ ArtResource, NY. © Artists Rights Society (ARS), New York. Reproduced by permission of Art Resource and Artists Rights Society (ARS), New York.

The Frieze of Life

During the 1890s, while living in Berlin and Paris, Munch produced his greatest works. His distinctive style is character-

ized by swirling lines, a dark and brooding atmosphere, and the frank depiction of such themes as fear, rage, desire, jealousy, love, and death. These themes were the central expressions of Munch's series of paintings known as *The Frieze of Life*. This series, first exhibited as a whole in Berlin in 1902, includes several smaller groupings of paintings that are linked by a similar subject matter.

Several of Munch's major works deal with his feelings about love, passion, and jealousy, and the uneasy relationship he had with women. Munch had several troubled affairs with women throughout his life, which led him to believe that a true union between two people was impossible. He also felt that a relationship—particularly a physical one—with a woman would undermine his creative expression. In Munch's painting *The Kiss,* a man and a woman passionately embrace. Their facial features blend into one another, which can be interpreted either as a sign of a potent union between lovers or a reflection of the capacity of love to swallow individual identities. In *Jealousy,* Munch depicts his friend, poet Stanislaw Przybyszewski (1868–1927), as the unhappy victim of an unfaithful woman. The poet's wife, Dagny Juell, is shown in the background dressed in red, a color representing her adultery. She stands talking to another man with one hand secretively behind her back while the other reaches for an apple, a reference to the biblical Eve causing the expulsion of Adam and Eve from the Garden of Eden.

Some of Munch's most disturbing paintings reflect his fascination with and fear of death. *Death in the Sickroom* arouses feelings of grief, despair, and loneliness. The viewer does not see the person who has died; this work focuses on the loved ones who, all in their own way, mourn their loss. The stooped postures of the people and the dark, brooding colors give a sense of the stifling presence of death in the room. Perhaps even more disturbing than Munch's paintings that deal specifically with death are his works that express a general feeling of intense, overwhelming anxiety. Munch's most famous work, *The Scream,* embodies this feeling of anguish. The terrified figure in the foreground stands with his hands over his ears to drown out what critic Ian Dunlop calls "the scream of nature." Two figures amble along on the bridge behind him, apparently oblivious to both the man's fear and the circumstance that caused it. Beneath the bridge stretches a dark, swirling body of water, and above it is an oppressive, red sky. In his diary, Munch recalled the event that inspired this work. While walking with friends in Norway one evening, Munch witnessed a dramatic sunset that triggered in him a sense of acute anxiety. He wrote: "I stood there trembling with fright, and I felt a loud, unending scream piercing nature."

Many of the subjects Munch treated in his paintings recurred in his graphic art, which included such methods of

Masterworks

1885–86	*The Sick Child*
1891–93	*Evening (The Yellow Boat)*
c. 1892	*Death in the Sickroom*
c. 1893	*Puberty*
1893	*The Scream*
1893–94	*The Vampire*
1895	*The Scream (lithograph)*
1895–1902	*Madonna*
c. 1899	*Girls on the Jetty*
1940–42	*Self-Portrait, Between Clock and Bed*

printmaking as woodcuts, lithographs, and etchings. His printmaking enabled him to experiment with different textures and styles while still exploring the themes that preoccupied him. In fact, *The Sick Child* and *The Scream* were just two of his subjects that appeared first as paintings and later as prints. Because the printing process enabled him to generate multiple copies, images he produced this way could also be distributed to a large audience. Munch's extensive work in this field had a huge impact on the development of modern graphic art.

A nervous breakdown

Munch had always struggled to keep his anxiety under control, and in 1908, aggravated by years of hard drinking, his mental condition took a turn for the worse. He had a nervous breakdown and spent eight months in a sanatorium in Denmark. After his release, he moved back to Norway where he stayed, except for occasional travel, for the rest of his life. His work underwent a dramatic change after that period: while still dramatic and thoughtful, his paintings were no longer intensely personal. He kept to subjects that were less provocative and less painful than his angst-ridden works from before his breakdown. He painted numerous self-portraits, as well as such everyday subjects as farmers and laborers at work and the Norwegian landscape. In 1909, the University of Oslo honored Munch with a commission to paint a set of murals, which were installed in 1916.

While the change in the tone of his works may indicate a newfound peace, Munch remained a lonely, isolated figure for the rest of his life. After Adolf Hitler (1889–1945) and the Nazis rose to power in Germany in the 1930s, dozens of Munch's paintings were labeled "degenerate," or morally disgusting, and removed from public view. The Nazis invaded

Norway in 1940, and Munch's final years were spent quietly avoiding the hated foreign rulers. Late in 1943, a nearby explosion shattered the windows of Munch's home. Disturbed by the event, he went out into the snow for a long walk. He came down with a bad cold that turned into bronchitis, which eventually killed the eighty-year-old artist. In his will, he left all of the works in his possession to the city of Oslo, which erected the Munch Museet (Munch Museum) to house them.

For More Information

Books

Dunlop, Ian. *Edvard Munch.* New York: St. Martin's Press, 1977.

Faerna, José María, ed. *Munch.* New York: Harry N. Abrams, Inc., 1996.

Messer, Thomas M. *Edvard Munch* (Masters of Art series). New York: Harry N. Abrams, Inc., 1986.

Web Sites

"Edvard Munch." *Mark Harden's Artchive.* [Online] Available http://www.artchive.com/artchive/M/munch.html (last accessed on July 3, 2001).

"Edvard Munch." *CGFA.* [Online] Available http://sunsite.dk/cgfa/munch/ (last accessed on July 3, 2001).

"Munch and Symbolism." *Nasjonalgalleriet Oslo.* [Online] Available http://www.museumsnett.no/nasjonalgalleriet/munch/eng/ (last accessed on July 3, 2001).

Yoko Ono

Born February 18, 1933
Tokyo, Japan

American musician and multimedia artist

B est known for her marriage to rock star John Lennon (1940–1980), Yoko Ono is an original artist whose long career has been marked by opposite extremes of controversy and simplicity. In the 1960s, she was a leader in the development of several experimental art forms, including conceptual art and performance art, and along the way she has had personal and professional associations with many artists, composers, and political activists. In addition, she has played a role in the evolution of pop music and experimental film. According to author Alexandra Munroe, "While her work has often confounded critics, her faith in the power of art to open and uplift the mind has touched millions."

From the time of Ono's 1969 marriage to Lennon through the breakup of his band, the Beatles, and his assassination in 1980, she became the subject of controversy and even mockery. Although it fit in with many of the trends in the New York art world, her art seemed strange and baffling to many of Lennon's fans. Furthermore, the determination to blend fame and pop music with her experimental art struck many people as opportunistic or pretentious. To her fans, however, Ono's perseverance honors Lennon's legacy and enables her to reach audiences who normally would not be exposed to art that challenges them intellectually.

Japanese beginnings

Yoko Ono's mother and father both came from families that made great fortunes in Japan's financial institutions. She was brought up in Tokyo amidst substantial wealth and traveled frequently to America. With her father's encouragement, she studied piano and voice. World War II (1939–45), however, interrupted daily life in Tokyo. Ono's father was assigned to Hanoi to manage the state bank, and her mother took care of her son and two daughters until the bombing of Tokyo prompted her to take them to a remote mountain village.

After the war, Ono resumed her education at Tokyo's Peers' School, where her classmates included a future emperor and Yukio Mishima (1925–1970), who would go on to become one of Japan's most important writers. Life in Tokyo was dominated by the U.S. military, and Ono was witness to her nation's slow and painful attempts to rebuild itself. In 1952, she was the first female student accepted into the philosophy program at Gakushuin University. There, she studied the tenets of Marxism, which focuses on the relations between people from an economic standpoint. Ono was also schooled in existentialism, a type of philosophy that centers on the question of setting priorities in a universe where there is no divine guidance. After two semesters, Ono left Gakushuin, moved with her family to New York, and signed up for classes at Sarah Lawrence University.

Joins the avant-garde

Ono's time at Sarah Lawrence was also brief. She married a composer named Ichiyanagi Toshi and got an apartment with him in New York City. Ichiyanagi was an associate of John Cage (1912–1992), a pivotal figure in New York's avant-garde

What Is the Avant-Garde?

A difficult term to define, the avant-garde (a French word that has entered the English dictionary) is generally associated with artists who experiment with new forms and challenge the way things are normally done. In 1939, critic Clement Greenberg wrote, "The avant-garde poet or artist tries in effect to imitate God by creating something valid solely on its own terms." This description captures the ambition and the seriousness of avant-gardism. In fact, one of the most frequent complaints about the avant-garde is that it takes itself too seriously. Nevertheless, a great many new ideas in theater, poetry, music, and the visual arts originated with avant-garde artists, before gradually entering mainstream or popular culture.

Historians agree that artists have not always adopted the confrontational stance of the avant-garde, but there is debate about when it exactly it arose. Many experts point to nineteenth-century France, where writer Gustave Flaubert (pronounced flo-BARE, 1821–1880) and painter Gustave Courbet (pronounced cor-BAY, 1819–1877) stirred up controversy with their proclamations and their work. Other avant-garde movements that have had a lasting effect on the art world include the Dadaists, a group of painters and performers active in Zurich, Switzerland, in the 1920s; and the circle of artists and musicians associated with John Cage, the American composer whose books, lectures, and performances promoted new approaches that initially struck people as bizarre. For example, Cage altered the way pianos sound by attaching clamps and screws to the strings inside. Nam June Paik (1932 –), one of Cage's followers, was the first artist to create works in the medium of video—preceding MTV by several decades.

music scene with connections to visual artists as well. To be "avant-garde" means to challenge "normal" ideas about art and to offer new, provocative ideas in their place. Ono recognized a kindred spirit in Cage, whose most famous composition, *4'33",* consisted of the pianist sitting at the piano and *not playing* for four minutes and thirty-three seconds. Cage was also involved in "happenings," performances where, for example, a dancer might move among the audience while a poet simultaneously read aloud in another part of the room and somebody else showed slides on the wall. Although not everybody took Cage's ideas seriously, an art movement called Fluxus formed in New York in the late 1950s and advocated similarly unexpected approaches to the process of making and showing art.

Ono joined Fluxus, contributing artworks in the form of instructions. *Lighting Piece,* performed in New York in 1961 and Tokyo in 1962, instructed: "Light a match and watch till it goes out." As a musician, she experimented with unusual vocal techniques and sound collages, or audiotapes featuring an array of sounds produced by musical instruments or recorded from daily life. Instead of painting on canvas, she wrote out instructions such as *Painting to See the Skies* (1962): "Drill two holes into a canvas. Hang it where you can see the sky." Critics cite Ono's so-called instruction paintings as landmarks in the development of conceptual art. This art form centers on ideas more than appearances, although the handwriting (she produced instructions in English and Japanese) has a simple and self-consciously artistic appearance. Ono's conceptual work is gathered in a book titled *Grapefruit,* which she has published in editions of various sizes between 1964 and 2000.

By 1963, Ono's marriage to Ichiyanagi had ended, and she married and had a daughter with Anthony Cox, an American artist. A restless soul, she moved between Tokyo, New York, and London for the next several years, creating artwork that continued to defy description, some of it produced with members of Fluxus and some independently. Three times between 1964 and 1966, in three different cities, she mounted a performance titled *Cut Piece.* For this work, she sat quietly on stage while members of the audience took turns cutting her clothes away with a pair of scissors. This ordeal made her feel both extremely vulnerable and deeply connected to the audience. Many people who witnessed *Cut Piece* or saw film footage of it realized that a new art form, known as performance art, had come into existence. While art usually involves *making* something, performance art involves *doing* something. Performance artists who have followed in Ono's footsteps include **Laurie Anderson** (1950–; see entry in volume 3) and Meredith Monk (1943–).

Meets John Lennon

London's Indica Gallery held an exhibition of Ono's work in November 1966. The works on view included *Painting to Hammer a Nail,* consisting of a white wood panel, a hammer, and a jar of nails (viewers were invited to pound nails into the panel); *Painting to Let the Evening Light Go Through,* a clear piece of Plexiglas; and *Ceiling Painting.* Also known as *Yes Painting,* this artwork comprised a ladder, a magnifying glass, and a glass panel bolted to the ceiling. When viewers climbed the ladder and looked through the magnifying glass, they could read the word *YES* printed in small letters on the panel. One of the visitors to the Indica Gallery was John Lennon, a member of the Beatles, the phenomenally popular 1960s band. Lennon, particularly impressed with the positive message of *Ceiling Painting,* sought Ono out, and in time a romance developed, leading to marriage in 1969.

Lennon's fame brought tremendous attention to Ono, whose work had previously been known only in avant-garde circles. His work with the Beatles immediately reflected her influence, especially the sound collage "Revolution No. 9" on the 1968 *The Beatles* album (popularly called *The White Album*). Lennon and Ono released an album of sonic experiments together titled *Unfinished Music No. 1: Two Virgins,* which featured nude photographs of the couple on the front and back cover. It was the first of many scandals to surround them. With a performance called *Bed-In for Peace* at the Amsterdam Hilton Hotel in March 1969 (repeated in Montreal in May), they learned how to use the press to spread their opinions about art and politics. Newspaper and television reporters came to the hotel room to do stories on the famous couple, who, instead of hiding, invited them in and discussed how love and peace could form the basis of a new utopia, or ideal society. At the time, America was involved in a war in the Southeast Asian country of Vietnam, and Lennon and Ono joined the protests against the government. In twelve different cities, they put up billboards reading "War Is Over If You Want It."

In 1969, creative differences between Lennon and the other Beatles led to the breakup of the band, an event that many fans

blamed on Ono. She endured years of public criticism and jokes that carried undertones of sexism and racism. Subsequent collaborations between Ono and Lennon included recordings, performances, and films, notably *Fly* (1970), which follows the title insect as it takes off from and lands on different parts of a woman's naked body. Their films do not have plots like Hollywood movies do; rather, like the films created by pop artist Andy Warhol (1928–1987; see entry in volume 2), they explore a single subject without offering commentary or explanation. Ono had made a film in 1966 titled *Bottoms,* which showed a series of unclothed, unidentified rear ends. This film was conceived as a plea for world peace—the idea being that wars would not be fought if people realized how much they had in common. Ono and Lennon had a son, Sean, in 1975, and their personal and artistic lives remained entwined throughout the 1970s. This extraordinarily close relationship ended on December 8, 1980, when John Lennon was murdered by a deranged fan.

Life after Lennon

Beyond her own feelings of grief and anger, Ono felt a responsibility to assist Lennon's millions of fans in their grief, too. She asked for ten minutes of silence to be observed on

Masterworks

1964–66	*Cut Piece*
1964–2000	*Grapefruit*
1966	*Bottoms*
	Ceiling Painting (Yes Painting)
1969	*War Is Over* (with John Lennon)
	Bed-In for Peace (with John Lennon)
1970	*Fly* (with John Lennon)
1980	Moment of silence for John Lennon
1985	*Strawberry Fields*
1992	*Onobox*

December 14, 1980. One hundred thousand people attended the vigil in New York's Central Park, and hundreds of radio stations offered their own silent tributes. Critics have classified this experience as one of Ono's bravest and most moving works of art. On October 9, 1985, the day that Lennon would have turned forty-five years old, Ono unveiled *Strawberry Fields* (the title comes from one of Lennon's songs with the Beatles), an area in Central Park marked off by trees contributed by countries from all over the world. A circle on the ground is inscribed with the word *Imagine* (another Lennon song title). This tribute has become one of New York's most visited spots. Over the course of the 1980s, Ono recorded a few albums and showed sculpture and other work in New York art galleries but generally stayed away from the spotlight. Her public image as Lennon's widow overshadowed her vital career as an artist.

In 1989, nearly a decade after Lennon's death, the Whitney Museum of American Art mounted a retrospective of Ono's art from her days with Fluxus to her series of bronze sculptures based on earlier work. The show was well received by critics and a public who had previously been skeptical about Ono's talent, and since that time, young musicians and artists have been rediscovering her challenging and often bizarre body of work. The 1992 release of *Onobox,* a collection of her recordings, was hailed as "a lost chapter in rock history," and the warm reception encouraged her to record and tour again, this time with a band that included Sean Lennon.

For More Information

Books
Hopkins, Jerry. *Yoko Ono.* New York: Macmillan, 1986.

Munroe, Alexandra, and Jon Hendricks, eds. *YES Yoko Ono.* New York: Japan Society and Harry N. Abrams, 2000.

Web Sites

AIU: A Yoko Ono Box. [Online] Available http://www. kaapeli.fi/aiu/ (last accessed on July 3, 2001).

Instant Karma! The John and Yoko Magazine Since 1981. [Online] Available http://www.instantkarma.com (last accessed on July 3, 2001).

Onoweb. [Online] Available http://www.metatronpress.com/ onoweb/ (last accessed on July 3, 2001).

I. M. Pei

Born April 26, 1917
Canton (Guangzhou), China

American architect

UPDATE

"Architects . . . search for that special quality that is the spirit of the place as no building exists alone."

Among the best-known architects in the world, I. M. Pei has designed numerous significant buildings. Rather than pursue a single architectural style, Pei has chosen to conform the design for each building to the particulars of the place it will occupy. His fondness, however, for such materials as glass and concrete, as well as a modernist approach, have lent a consistent look to many of his structures. **(See original entry on Pei in volume 2.)**

Perhaps most renowned for his expansion of the world-famous Louvre museum (called Le Grand Louvre after Pei's expansion and renovation) in Paris, France, Pei has displayed a passion for bold geometrical shapes and dramatic contrasts throughout his career. When Pei first unveiled plans to erect a huge glass pyramid in the courtyard of the stately seventeenth-century Louvre, a number of critics expressed outrage, feeling the pyramid's ultramodern design was an inappropriate addition to the elegance of the museum. Pei's supporters won out, however, and his pyramid—a Paris landmark—is praised for its grace and simplicity. Pei has described the project as "the greatest challenge and the greatest accomplishment of my career."

Born Ieoh Ming Pei in 1917, the Harvard-educated architect has designed dozens of structures that have served many different purposes, from public housing to corporate headquarters to university buildings and hospitals. The designs that have won him the most acclaim have been those of museums throughout the world. A few years before he was hired to design the expansion and renovation of the Louvre, Pei created an addition to another important museum, the National Gallery of Art in Washington, D.C. His east wing, completed in 1978, successfully met the challenge of creating a new, updated structure that blended harmoniously with the existing west wing of the museum. For the new wing, Pei used marble from the same quarry that had supplied materials for the original building. The two triangular structures of the east wing are connected by a large atrium; its open architecture allows for an easy flow of the museum's visitors in a spacious, skylit structure. The American Institute of Architects elected Pei's east wing as one of the ten best buildings in the United States.

Rock and roll and ancient art

To prepare for the design of the Rock and Roll Hall of Fame and Museum in Cleveland, Ohio, Pei immersed himself in the music, which he acknowledged had been mostly unfamiliar to him. Before he began work on the museum, which opened in 1995, Pei visited Graceland, the former home of Elvis Presley; traveled to New Orleans to learn firsthand about jazz and blues; and attended several rock concerts. His design for the waterfront structure, with its dramatic, angular shape and modern style, conveys the bold and youthful energy of rock and roll. Echoing some of his other famous buildings, particularly the Louvre expansion, the Hall of Fame and Museum includes a huge triangular glass "tent" connected to a seven-story tower. A wing of the building containing a theater juts out

◀ *I. M. Pei. Reproduced by permission of AP/ Wide World Photos.*

over Lake Erie, and visitors can attend outdoor concerts on the roof of the main building. Designing the building to maximize natural light and foster a sense of openness, Pei filled the interior of the glass tent with open balconies, bridges, and escalators.

In contrast to Pei's high-profile urban structures, the Miho Museum outside of Kyoto, Japan, is located in a remote mountain setting, barely visible from the road leading to it. Completed in 1997, the Miho Museum was built in the midst of a nature preserve, and Pei had to follow strict specifications to ensure that the building blended in with the serene beauty of the environment. To follow these specifications, Pei designed the structure so that eighty percent of it is underground. As Janet Koplos describes in *Art in America* magazine, Pei "excavated the top of a mountain, erected a building, and put the mountain back." The rooftops, made of glass and aluminum, are distinctly modern in their materials, yet they recall tradi-

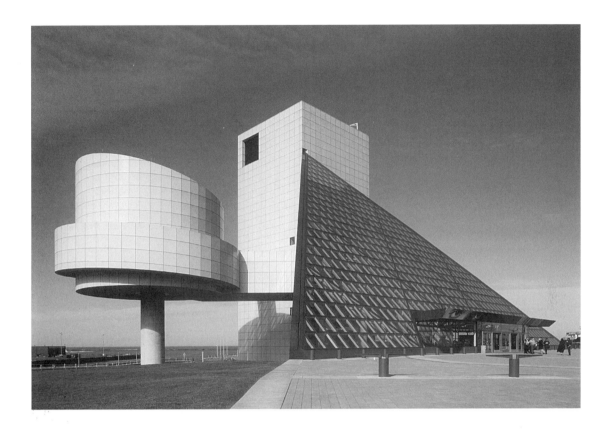

tional Japanese architecture in their style. Containing an impressive display of ancient art owned by a Japanese religious order called Shinji Shumeikai, the Miho Museum is reached after a walk on a winding path, through a tunnel, over a bridge, and up a staircase. "Detachment from the world," Pei has said, "is the most important element in this design."

In addition to being renowned among the general public, Pei has won numerous awards for his architecture. In 1979, he was awarded the American Institute of Architects Gold Medal, the highest architectural honor in the United States. (See box for information about another leading contemporary architect, Michael Graves.) He won the prestigious Pritzker Architecture Prize in 1983, using the $100,000 award to establish a scholarship fund for Chinese architecture students who wish to study in the United States. He received two medals from the U.S. government: the Medal of Liberty in 1986 and the Medal of Freedom in 1990. And in 1998, Pei was announced the winner

The Rock and Roll Hall of Fame Museum in Cleveland Ohio. Designed by I. M. Pei (early 1990s). Photograph, © Bill Ross. Reproduced by permission of the Corbis Corporation.

Michael Graves

The web site of Michael Graves and Associates, www.michaelgraves.com, highlights Graves's four principal interests: planning (that is, the development of architectural programs involving more than one building and the landscapes between them), architecture, interior design, and product design. Graves's most popular products include a sleek tea kettle for Alessi and a whimsical toaster for Target.

Born in Indianapolis, Indiana, in 1934, Graves studied architecture at the University of Cincinnati and Harvard University. In 1972, he joined the faculty at Princeton University, and around this time he began working in a style termed postmodern. Postmodernism in architecture means intentionally breaking the rules set down by the modern architects of the twentieth century and blending past styles with futuristic materials and technologies. Both these tendencies are apparent in Graves's designs for the Swan and Dolphin hotels in Florida's Disney World. He continues to live and work in Princeton, New Jersey.

Graves won the 2001 Gold Medal from the American Institute of Architects (see www.aia.org), and today

Michael Graves. Photograph by Bernard Gotfryd. Reproduced by permission of Archive Photos.

is considered one of the leading architects of the early twenty-first century, along with figures such as I. M. Pei, Philippe Starck (1949–), and Frank Gehry (1929–). Although they work in different styles, Graves, Starck, and Gehry all believe that their profession encompasses not just buildings but also furniture and other products.

of the distinguished Edward MacDowell Medal for outstanding contributions to the arts; he is the only architect to have received the award.

For More Information

Books and Periodicals

Boehm, Gero Von. *Conversations with I. M. Pei: Light Is the Key.* New York: Prestel USA, 2000.

Dietsch, Deborah K. "Hidden Paradise." *Architecture* 87 (January 1998): p. 82.

Koplos, Janet. "The Hidden Museum." *Art in America* 86 (November 1998): p. 50.

Reid, Aileen. *I. M. Pei.* New York: Knickerbocker Press, 1998.

Wiseman, Carter. *I. M. Pei: A Profile in American Architecture.* New York: Harry N. Abrams, Inc., 1990.

Web Sites

"Ieoh Ming Pei." *The Pritzker Architecture Prize.* [Online] Available http://www.pritzkerprize.com/pei.htm (last accessed May 29, 2001).

"I. M. Pei." *The Great Buildings Collection.* [Online] Available http://www.great-buildings.com/architects/I._M._Pei.html (last accessed May 29, 2001).

Miho Museum. [Online] Available http://www.miho.or.jp/index.html (last accessed May 29, 2001).

Pei Cobb Freed & Partners. [Online] Available http://www.pcfandp.com/a/p/8704/s.html (last accessed May 29, 2001).

Masterworks

1967	National Center for Atmospheric Research, Boulder, Colorado
1978	National Gallery of Art, East Wing, Washington, D. C.
1979	John F. Kennedy Library, Boston, Massachusetts
1982	Fragrant Hill Hotel, Beijing, China
1984	Bank of China, Hong Kong
1989	Le Grand Louvre (expansion), Paris, France
	Meyerson Symphony Center, Dallas, Texas
1993	Le Grand Louvre (renovation), Paris, France
1995	Rock and Roll Hall of Fame and Museum, Cleveland, Ohio
1997	Miho Museum, Shigaraki, Japan

Camille Pissarro

Born July 10, 1830
Charlotte Amalie, St. Thomas

Died November 12, 1903
Paris, France

French painter

> "[J]ust think among other instances of the impressionists who would have been able to achieve a real synthesis if the young men had been able to earn a livelihood with some ease."
>
> Camille Pissarro, letter to his son, Lucien

A founder of impressionism, the once-radical school of painting that achieved wide popularity and influence in subsequent years, Camille Pissarro created vibrant paintings of Paris and the countryside. He played an important role in promoting impressionism's novel approach to sunlight, movement, and subject matter, among other issues, and kept faith in the style through long years of frustration. As a Jewish artist active in a climate of pervasive anti-Semitism, Pissarro was sensitive to political injustice of all kinds, and while this sentiment does not seem to come across in his paintings, it colored his life and perhaps accounted for his fierce determination.

Island beginnings

Although he came to be known for his vivid scenes of France, Camille Pissarro was born on the Caribbean island of

St. Thomas. This island is now part of the U.S. Virgin Islands and a popular vacation spot, but then it was a Danish colony known for its active harbor and its religious tolerance. The artist's uncle had a clothing store, and when he died, Frédéric Pissarro, the artist's father, moved to the island, eventually marrying the uncle's widow. Jacob Camille Pissarro was the third of their four sons.

When he was eleven years old, Pissarro was sent to a boarding school outside of Paris. Although he was expected to follow his father into business, drawing lessons and visits to the Louvre museum interested him much more. Nevertheless, when he returned home he obeyed his parents' wishes—for about four years. In 1852, at the age of twenty-two, Pissarro and a Danish artist named Fritz Melbye hopped a ship bound for Caracas, Venezuela. The relatively lively cultural environment appealed to Pissarro, and he set up a studio and began making portraits and capturing scenes of the marketplace. Slavery was abolished in Venezuela in 1854, and this event helped form the artist's social consciousness. His own family had owned slaves back in St. Thomas, but Pissarro came to believe that slavery was morally wrong, and in time his politics would grow radical.

Seeks his destiny in Paris

In the 1800s, Paris had one of the most vital art scenes in the world. In addition to the Louvre, a museum where many of the most famous paintings in the Western world could be found, there were the exhibitions known as "salons" mounted by the prestigious Academy of Fine Arts, and, in 1855, there was the Universal Exhibition. Highlighting France's commerce and industry, the Universal Exhibition also featured an art exhibition of more than five thousand paintings and sculptures. Pissarro arrived in November, in time to catch the last few days of the Universal Exhibition. Of all the art on display, he was most impressed with that of Camille Corot (pronounced ko-RO, 1796–1875), whose large imaginary landscapes and studies of humble farmers had attracted a small group of admirers, including the emperor, Napoleon III (1808–1873).

◀ Self Portrait (1873). Painting by Camille Pissarro. Musée d'Orsay, Paris, France. Photograph, © Archivo Iconografico, S.A. Reproduced by permission of the Corbis Corporation.

Pissarro sought out Corot, who encouraged him to view the natural scenery outside of Paris. The tropical landscapes of St. Thomas and Caracas continued to cloud Pissarro's vision, however, and he often painted these scenes from memory until he grew accustomed to his new surroundings. Anton Melbye, the cousin of his Venezuelan companion, employed him to paint the skies of Melbye's own landscape pictures. In addition, Pissarro enrolled in private art classes. He was determined to make up for his lack of early formal training, without sacrificing the unique perspective afforded him by the years he spent in the Caribbean.

Two events in 1859 spurred Pissarro's development as an artist. First, he submitted a painting to the Academy titled *Landscape at Montmorency,* and it was exhibited in that year's salon. The painting, now lost, attracted little attention. Second, he met and befriended Claude Monet (1840–1926; see entry in volume 2). Ten years younger than Pissarro, Monet shared his admiration for Corot and his determination to paint directly from nature. At a time when most nature scenes were painted indoors, from memory, this was a bold choice. Throughout their long friendship, Pissarro and Monet had many disagreements over matters artistic and personal, but they always admired each other's work.

A rebellious temperament

Although the term *impressionism* did not come into existence until 1874, the first stirrings of this movement date back to the 1860s, when Pissarro, Monet, and other artists, including Paul Cézanne (1839–1906; see entry in volume 1), Alfred Sisley (1839–1899), and Pierre-Auguste Renoir (pronounced ren-WAHR, 1841–1919; see entry in volume 2) found each other and exchanged ideas about where French painting might go next. They objected to the dictatorial rule of the Academy of Fine Arts and sought new techniques and subjects to clear away the staleness fostered by decades of academic painting.

At the same time, the artists continued submitting work to the very institution they opposed. Pissarro's *Banks of the*

Marne, Winter was accepted for the 1866 salon. A sparse landscape showing a woman and child walking along a path away from a simple farmhouse, it elicited these words from thÉmile Zola (1840–1902), a friend of the artist through Cézanne: "A grave and austere kind of painting, an extreme care for truth and rightness, an iron will. You are a clumsy blunderer, sir— you are an artist that I like." This review was not the kind of praise that attracted buyers. The next year, neither Pissarro nor any of his companions gained acceptance into the salon.

In the background of this professional rebellion, Pissarro rebelled against his family by having a relationship with Julie Vellay starting in 1860. (They did not marry until ten years later.) Vellay, a servant of Pissarro's mother and father, had left St. Thomas for the Paris suburb of Passy. Pissarro's relationship with Vellay did not meet with parental approval because of her position and because she was not Jewish. Their disapproval somewhat softened, however, after Vellay gave birth to the first of eight children. Frédéric Pissarro died in 1865, and the artist's continued failure to sell his work left him financially dependent on his mother, who never fully accepted Vellay into the family.

Pissarro did not share his parents' religious feelings and parted ways from their political viewpoint, too. He picked up radical ideas from the contemporary authors he read, including anarchists Pyotr Kropotkin (1842–1921) and Pierre-Joseph Proudhon (1809–1865). Anarchism, a school of thought that opposes authority and law, was exemplified by Proudhon's rallying cry "Property is theft."

The difficult birth of impressionism

Starting in 1869, Pissarro and his family lived in Louveciennes, a small town near Paris on the way to the Palace of Versailles. Monet was there, too, and the two painters were extremely productive, averaging a painting a week. Sometimes they selected the same view to paint; Pissarro's *Road to Versailles at Louveciennes—Rain Effect* and Monet's *Road to Versailles at Louveciennes—Snow Effect,* both from 1870, show the artists moving toward a spontaneous and sensitive approach to capturing the subtleties of light, shadow, and atmosphere in a landscape.

The war between France and Prussia (Franco-Prussian War, 1870–71) made it unsafe to remain in Louveciennes, so Pissarro, Monet, and their families relocated to London until the situation improved. It turns out they left just in time to save themselves, but Prussian forces destroyed many of the Pissarro paintings that were left behind. While in London, the artists saw work by such English artists as J. M. W. Turner (1775–1851; see entry in volume 2) and John Constable (1776–1837), which inspired them to even greater freedoms in their quest to transfer the constantly shifting natural world onto canvas.

Back in France, the artists found the judges of academic art to be as conservative as ever. In 1873, Pissarro, Monet, Renoir, and twelve other artists formed a cooperative partnership for exhibiting their work. When their first show opened April 15 of the following year, the critical and popular response was harsh. Focusing on Pissarro's *Hoar-Frost,* Louis Leroy, the journalist who invented the term *impressionism* as an insult, asked: "Those are furrows? That is hoar-frost? But those are palette-scrapings placed uniformly on a dirty canvas. It has neither head nor tail, neither top nor bottom, neither front nor back." The artists who participated in the first impressionist exhibition had been optimistic about winning the public over and were surprised at this unwelcome reaction. The cooperative partnership was dissolved.

The core group of artists mounted seven more exhibitions through 1886. Dealer Paul Durand-Ruel organized these shows, while Pissarro helped maintain the sometimes fragile alliance holding the painters together. For the most part, impressionism continued to attract scorn and ridicule. An increasing number of artists, however, began to take notice of and to sympathize with the impressionists. Among this second wave of impressionists were Paul Gauguin (pronounced go-GAN; 1848–1903; see entry in volume 1), Gustave Caillebotte (pronounced KY-bot; 1848–1894), and Mary Cassatt (1844–1926; see entry in volume

The Boulevard Montmartre: Afternoon, Sunshine *(1897)*. *Painting by Camille Pissarro.* Oil on canvas. 74 x 92.8 cm. The State Hermitage Museum, St. Petersburg, Russia.

1), and as the movement grew, the shock and hostility showed signs of subsiding. At the same time, the artists practicing "impressionism" started going in so many stylistic directions that the term became hard to define. Pissarro and Gauguin had a particularly troubled relationship, because Gauguin, a former stockbroker, had numerous ideas for improving sales that in Pissarro's view would have undermined the idealistic intentions behind the art.

Focuses on his own career

As the chief "ambassador" of the impressionists, Pissarro often took responsibility for settling the artistic and personal

Jackson Pollock

Born January 28, 1912
Cody, Wyoming

Died August 11, 1956
Southampton, New York

American painter

UPDATE

"When I am in my painting, I'm not aware of what I'm doing."

▲ *Jackson Pollack.*
© 2000 Pollock-Krasner Foundation / Artists Rights Society (ARS), New York. Reproduced by permission of Artists Rights Society, Inc.

Jackson Pollock's startlingly original paintings are credited with giving America an artistic style suited to its passion for freedom. Pollock and the other artists associated with abstract expressionism, also known as the New York school, attracted worldwide attention with their sometimes controversial work. As with anything truly original, abstract expressionism was greeted with hostility at first, with critics accusing its practitioners of giving in to utter chaos. A few people, however, recognized Pollock's genius for balancing what seemed to be total disorganization with rigid control. In subsequent decades, the innovations of the abstract expressionists have profoundly influenced music and literature in addition to the visual arts. **(See original entry on Pollock in volume 2.)**

Abstract expressionism was an American art movement that involved the energetic application of paint on the canvas. As the most famous abstract expressionist, Pollock has long been the focus of biographers and critics attempting to come to terms with the movement's impact. Along the way, his life has been examined in as great detail as his paintings. Depressed, alcoholic, and aggressive, Pollock's personality became well-known through a prizewinning biography in 1991, which inspired a feature film in 2000. While some of Pollock's fans consider the emphasis on the artist's life to be a distraction from serious inquiry into his work, it is undeniable that the fame of the book and movie has brought his work to the attention of many people who would not normally see it.

Leads a troubled life

Born in Wyoming and raised in California, Jackson Pollock moved to New York City in 1930. The city exposed him to the latest trends in modern art, in particular, the powerful political murals of David Alfaro Siqueiros (1896–1974) and the work of Wassily Kandinsky (1866–1944; see entry in volume 1), the Russian artist credited with producing the first abstract paintings. (Instead of showing a person, a landscape, or a still life, abstract paintings present forms and colors that do not resemble anything in the physical world.) For years, as Pollock struggled to arrive at an original style, he simultaneously struggled to control his alcoholism. The treatment known as psychoanalysis helped with both issues, helping the artist to explore the causes of his unhappiness and the motives behind his ambitions as a painter. The drawings Pollock made for his psychoanalyst in the late 1930s have become important to studies of his artistic evolution.

Even more helpful with Pollock's personal troubles was his wife Lee Krasner (1908–1984), a Brooklyn-born painter sympathetic to his artistic concerns and committed to his career, even at the expense of her own. Krasner arranged for exhibitions of Pollock's work, promoted it with critics and curators, and moved with him out of the city to East Hampton, a small community on Long Island. It was in the shed behind their Long Island home that Pollock did his best work, especially between 1947 and 1950 when he made a noteworthy change in his method: laying the canvas flat on the floor instead of propping it up on an easel. Works he produced during this period,

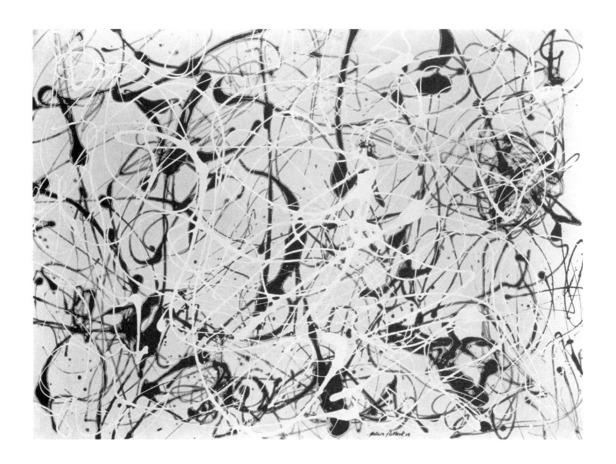

Number 23, 1948 *(1948)*.
*Painting by Jackson
Pollock*. Reproduced by
permission of Art Resource.

including *Number 23, 1948* and *Autumn Rhythm: Number 30, 1950,* have had a substantial impact on musicians, writers, as well as other artists searching for ways to express themselves with force and immediacy. American novelist Jack Kerouac (1922–1969), for example, drew inspiration from Pollock when he typed his *On the Road* (1957) on a single roll of paper.

The productive years between 1947 and 1950 approximately coincided with an interruption in Pollock's alcoholic tendencies, but eventually he started drinking again. Pollock was drunk when he crashed his car in the summer of 1956, killing himself and one of his two passengers. As with James Dean (1931–1955), the popular American actor who had died in a car crash one year earlier, Pollock became more famous after his death, and both men came to personify an artistic and personal recklessness that is at once dangerous and powerfully appealing.

His fame grows

Pollock's reputation continued to widen during the 1960s, 1970s, and 1980s, as his work gained acceptance among those who initially objected to it. Additionally, subsequent artists found inspiration in his painting style. In 1991, Steven Naifeh and Gregory White Smith wrote *Jackson Pollock: An American Saga,* and it went on to win the prestigious Pulitzer Prize. This well-researched and highly detailed biography boosted the artist's reputation, focusing attention on his personal troubles. For several years, American actor Ed Harris, who bears a superficial resemblance to Pollock, planned to make a movie based on the book, and in preparation for this role he took extensive painting lessons.

Harris's movie, titled *Pollock,* came out in 2000 to critical acclaim. Audiences responded to Marcia Gay Harden's portrayal of Krasner, the woman who recognized Pollock's talent and made great sacrifices to boost his career. As if to make up for the lack of attention Krasner had received as an artist during her lifetime, the Brooklyn Museum of Art held a retrospective of her career in 2000; the exhibition highlighted the work she created in the decades following her husband's death.

Masterworks	
1938–40	The psychoanalytic drawings
1948	*Number 23, 1948*
1950	*Lavender Mist: Number 1, 1950*
	Autumn Rhythm, Number 30, 1950
1952	*Blue Poles: Number 11, 1952*

For More Information

Books

Naifeh, Steven, and Gregory White Smith. *Jackson Pollock: An American Saga.* New York: HarperTrade, 1991.

Varnedoe, Kirk, and Pepe Karmel. *Jackson Pollock.* New York: The Museum of Modern Art, 1998.

Web Sites

"Jackson Pollock." *The Museum of Modern Art.* [Online] Availablehttp://www.moma.org/exhibitions/pollock/website100/ (last accessed on July 3, 2001).

"Jackson Pollock." *National Gallery of Art.* [Online] Available http://www.nga.gov/feature/pollock/pollockhome.html (last accessed on July 3, 2001).

"Pollock, Jackson." *WebMuseum, Paris.* [Online] Available http://www.ibiblio.org/wm/paint/auth/pollock/ (last accessed on July 3, 2001).

"Pollock-Krasner House & Study Center." *SUNY Stonybrook.* [Online] Available http://naples.cc.sunysb.edu/CAS/ pkhouse.nsf (last accessed on July 3, 2001).

Beatrix Potter

Born July 28, 1866
London, England
Died December 22, 1943
Sawrey, England

English author and illustrator

With her stories and illustrations relating the adventures of rabbits, mice, hedgehogs, and other animals, Potter became one of the most beloved children's authors of her era. Books such as *The Tale of Peter Rabbit* and *The Tale of Squirrel Nutkin* continue to engage children and adults, thanks to their creator's gentle sense of humor and storytelling ability. Potter loved animals and based several of her characters on her own pets. She kept a sheep farm in England's Lake District, balancing chores with creative activities for most of her life.

As an artist, Potter is best remembered for her delicate drawings with their amusing details and pleasing colors. Unlike the illustrations of Dr. Seuss (Theodor Geisel, 1904–1991; see box in Maurice Sendak entry in volume 4), for example, Potter's pictures always closely resembled real animals—although they wear clothes and walk upright. She enjoyed drawing from nature and created many such drawings

"I have never quite understood the secret of Peter's perennial charm."

▲ **Beatrix Potter.**
Reproduced by permission of Archive Photos.

for their own sake rather than as illustrations for a story. Flowers were a favorite subject, as were insects, and when she wanted to she could draw with scientific precision. The only subject she generally avoided drawing was human beings. Potter's art has taken on a life beyond her stories, as well, turning up as stuffed animals and on children's clothing.

Town and country

Rupert Potter, the son of a member of the English Parliament and successful merchant, had a love of drawing. Instead of pursuing an artistic career, however, he became a lawyer in London, where he married Helen Leech in 1863. They had a daughter, Helen Beatrix Potter, and a son, Walter Bertram Potter. As was the custom for wealthy families during this period in English history, the children were brought up largely by their nurse, or nanny. According to Beatrix Potter, the Scottish nurse in their household was a firm believer in witches and fairies, and the stories she told instilled in the children a fascination with the world of magic. Potter also remembered that when she turned ten years old, "my father gave me Mrs. Blackburn's book of birds, drawn from nature, for my birthday present." From that point, Beatrix Potter started down the path of the artistic career her father had sidestepped.

Potter also developed a love of reading from a young age, with the stories of Sir Walter Scott (1771–1832) being among her favorites. She and her brother, who was six years younger, shared an interest in animals and the natural world, and they always looked forward to trips to the countryside. Bolton Gardens, the family's London residence, was more luxurious than the homes of the vast majority of Londoners, and the Potters took two annual vacations. For two weeks every April, they went to the western part of Britain. And every year, from the end of July until the middle of October, the Potters vacationed at Dalguise House, a mansion in Perthshire, Scotland. Beatrix and Bertram went on long walks, collecting flowers and birds' eggs, and sometimes catching and taming rabbits. In addition to a loyal spaniel named Spot, the Potter children kept a great variety of pets, among them snakes, salamanders, newts, and even bats. Beatrix Potter made drawings of the pets and kept journals detailing their arrival, behavior patterns, sicknesses, and deaths. Because she did not trust her mother, she invented a cipher, or code, and, later in life, even Beatrix Potter herself could not decode her own journals. She enjoyed a better relationship with her father. In addition to being a lawyer, Rupert Potter was one of England's first photographers, and he took many portraits of his family as well such friends as Prime Minister William Gladstone (1809–1898), painter John Everett Millais (1829–1896), and minister and humanitarian William Gaskell (1805–1884), who was like an uncle to Beatrix Potter.

Dalguise was the ideal retreat for the family, but in 1882 the landlord raised the rent considerably, and Rupert Potter found another house: Wray's Castle, in England's Lake District. This region had long inspired poets and painters, and for the Potter children it meant new species of plants and animals to study and draw. Beatrix Potter developed a lifelong affection for the Lake District and would spend most of her adult years there.

A lonely existence

Potter suffered from poor health, however, and her parents, fearing germs, forbade her from playing with other children. Her closest companions were her brother, her grandmother on her father's side, and her various nurses and tutors. The last of these tutors, Annie Carter, who was only three years older than Potter, left the household in 1885 to get married to an engineer named Edwin Moore. To compensate for her loneliness, Potter had to come up with ways of entertaining herself. In addition to drawing, she wrote down stories about her pets and their adventures.

In 1890, Potter began submitting her drawings of rabbits to publishers of Christmas cards, and the firm of Hildesheimer & Faulkner bought a set. Later that year, the same company published *The Happy Pair,* a collection of

Illustration of Peter Rabbit by Beatrix Potter, from her The Tale of Peter Rabbit (1903). Public domain.

poems by Frederic E. Weatherly (1848–1929), with illustrations by "H.B.P."—Helen Beatrix Potter. These successes encouraged her to create a booklet of her own stories, but the publishers rejected her initial submissions. She continued inventing stories anyway, to amuse herself and those close to her. In 1893, she wrote and illustrated a letter to Noel Moore, one of the children of Annie Carter (now Annie Moore). The letter featured a rabbit named Peter.

Potter's artistic pastime took on a scientific aspect when she developed an interest in mushrooms and other fungi as well as lichen (the combination of algae and fungus). She made detailed drawings of specimens under the microscope, and in 1897 she published her findings on lichen with the Linnean Society, a British scientific organization. This accomplishment meant a lot to her because the all-male society initially discouraged her from submitting a paper.

Success and grief

In 1901, having endured a number of rejections from publishers, Potter took matters into her own hands and enlisted a printer called Strangeways & Sons to produce 250 copies of *The Tale of Peter Rabbit,* which was based on the letter she had written to Noel Moore eight years earlier. She gave away most copies as Christmas presents and sold a few of them. Receiving encouragement from her readers, including the creator of Sherlock Holmes, Arthur Conan Doyle (1859–1930), she printed another two hundred copies, and soon publisher F. W. Warne expressed interest in *Peter Rabbit.*

The company's founder, Frederick Warne (1825–1901), had died in 1901, and his son Norman handled many of the details involved with preparing the book for publication. He convinced Potter to redo her black-ink drawings in watercolor and they soon began work on two additional books: *The Tailor of Gloucester* and *The Tale of Squirrel Nutkin.* In the book's most memorable scene, squirrels make rafts from twigs and paddle across the water, using their tails as sails.

By the end of 1903, Warne had sold more than fifty thousand copies of *Peter Rabbit,* creating income for Potter far beyond her expectations. She used the money to buy property for herself in the Lake District, and she attempted to meet the demand for *Peter Rabbit* merchandise with a doll, wallpaper, and more. She also wrote and illustrated a "sequel" about Peter's cousin, Benjamin Bunny.

Potter greatly enjoyed her correspondence with Norman Warne, and in 1905 a very unusual letter came from her publisher: a proposal of marriage. Although she was thirty-nine years old, her parents still guided her life in many ways, and they objected to the union. Nevertheless, Potter accepted

Masterworks

1901	*The Tale of Peter Rabbit*
1903	*The Tailor of Gloucester*
	The Tale of Squirrel Nutkin
1905	*The Tale of Mrs. Tiggy-winkle*
1908	*The Tale of Jemima Puddle-Duck*

Warne's offer, coping with her family antagonisms by pouring her energy into the illustrations for *The Tale of Mrs. Tiggy-winkle.* This book, about a hedgehog who finds the pocket-handkerchiefs of a girl named Lucie, features detailed watercolors of flowers and household utensils. In September 1905, before a wedding could take place, Warne died of a blood disease. The loss was devastating for Potter.

Life on Hill Top

Over the years, the small piece of land Potter had bought for herself expanded to accommodate sheep, cows, pigs, ducks, and hens. On Hill Top Farm, as the property was called, Potter and a few assistants ignored twentieth-century conventions and used old-fashioned methods to care for the livestock. Hill Top often served as the setting of her books, notably *The Tale of Jemima Puddle-Duck,* who wears a bonnet and shawl and enlists the assistance of a collie named Kep (based on Potter's own favorite dog) in retrieving some of her eggs that a fox claims to be protecting.

Potter's time was divided between farming, writing and illustrating new books, and overseeing the creation of merchandise related to her stories, including dolls, board games, and tea sets. Handling all this business required the expertise of a lawyer. William Heelis helped her with legal matters, and in 1913, the lawyer and client were married. Rupert Potter died the next year, and the couple added looking after her mother to their many responsibilities.

Altogether, Potter wrote and illustrated twenty-three tales, all of which have been reprinted more than one hundred times. She managed this feat while maintaining the farm and campaigning for the protection of her beloved Lake District. Upon her death, the vast estate she had accumulated was turned over to the government, which has kept it operating as a public park.

A sizable collection of Potter's drawings and watercolors was given to London's Victoria and Albert Museum.

For More Information

Books

Denyer, Susan. *At Home with Beatrix Potter: The Creator of Peter Rabbit.* New York: Harry N. Abrams, 2000.

Taylor, Judy. *Beatrix Potter: Artist, Storyteller and Country-woman.* New York: Frederick Warne, 1986.

Web Sites

The Peter Rabbit Official Website. [Online] Available http://www.peterrabbit.co.uk/ (last accessed on July 3, 2001).

Martin Puryear

Born May 23, 1941
Washington, D.C.

American sculptor

"I use materials, ideas, movement and time to express a whole view of my art in the world."

Martin Puryear creates sculptures made of wood, stone, and other materials. Trained as a woodworker, he is an able craftsperson, and though his work assumes many forms, exceptional construction is a constant. Puryear is inspired by furniture, architecture, and crafts from around the world as well as great sculpture of his time, especially the work of the American minimalist movement, a school of art that found poetry in basic geometric shapes. He shares with this movement the appreciation of the texture and weight of wood and other materials, but unlike many other minimalists, he blends materials and often lets his sense of humor show. Puryear has made a great deal of outdoor work, some of it enormous in scale, notably *Bodark Arc,* a semicircular structure nearly four hundred feet in diameter.

Puryear plays with appearances, just as he plays with the materials he uses. It is often hard to say whether his sculptures are abstract or representational. That is, his work is often somewhere between the kind of sculpture that is only about shapes and forms and the kind of sculpture intended to represent an animal or something else in the world. Completed in 1987, one untitled work made of tar, steel mesh, and Douglas-fir may appear to some viewers as mouse with a curly tail, but others may just see a ring and part of a cone. At other times, shapes reminiscent of birds' heads, deer antlers, and animal bones may be identified, but there is always something else going on. Neal Benezra writes of this inventive American sculptor: "Puryear has strived to make his work one of possibilities and abundance."

Childhood curiosity leads in many directions

Reginald Puryear, a postal employee, and Martina Puryear, a schoolteacher, had seven children; and Martin was the eldest. He was very good at drawing, but initially he directed this skill not toward art but toward copying pictures of birds and insects. Hawks were an enduring interest, and he read everything he could find on the subject of falconry, the training of hawks to follow commands. He even made a hood for the hawk he hoped to catch one day, and later he returned to the hood shape in his sculpture.

In 1958, Puryear entered Catholic University in his hometown of Washington, D.C., where he planned on studying biology, the science of living things. After a few years of college, however, he decided to study art. Initially, he was only attracted to realistic painters from the past, but Nell Sonneman, a teacher at the school, helped Puryear to discover the philosophical basis for modern art. He started out as a painter, but by the time he graduated in 1963 he was determined to be a sculptor.

Travels the world

After college, Puryear joined the Peace Corps, an international organization dedicated to improving the living conditions in poor nations. He received a two-year assignment in Sierra Leone, in West Africa, where he taught biology, English, and French. As an African American, Puryear was interested in African culture and especially the woodworkers he met in

"If I became interested in archery, I made the bows and arrows; if I became interested in music, I made the guitar."

Martin Puryear, on his youth

Sierra Leone. He learned how they made furniture and other products without the aid of power tools. This journey was the first in a long series of trips great and small.

From Africa, Puryear moved to Stockholm, Sweden, and in 1967 he began taking classes at the Swedish Royal Academy of Art. This part of the world, known as Scandinavia, has a markedly different climate and landscape from both Africa and America, and, more important to his development as an artist, the craft of woodworking is extremely advanced. Puryear was so impressed with the work of James Krenov (1920–), a cabinetmaker born in Siberia, raised in Seattle, Washington, and living in Stockholm, that he spent a few weeks at his studio observing him. Another influence on Puryear during this period was Stockholm's vital art scene and its modern art museum. Before returning to the United States, he traveled to the Biennale, a large art fair in Venice, Italy. Here he saw the work of the Donald Judd (1928–1994), Tony Smith (1912–1981), and Robert Morris (1931–)—three of the foremost artists of America's minimalist movement.

New Haven, Nashville, and New York

In 1969, Puryear enrolled in the sculpture program at Yale University in New Haven, Connecticut. There, he studied with Morris and another important minimalist, Richard Serra (1939 –; see box). The minimalists generally believed that steel, wood, and other materials were interesting in their own right, and therefore it was not necessary to mold or carve them into elaborate shapes. Minimalists limited themselves to cubes and other simple forms. Although Puryear has gone on to produce works that are not strictly minimalist, the appreciation for materials has stayed with him throughout his career.

After Yale, Puryear taught art at Fisk University, an African American college in Nashville, Tennessee. This environment, closer to the American heartland, perhaps motivated him to use more natural materials such as rope, leather, and rawhide in his sculptures.

By 1973, however, he wanted to be closer to New York's fast-paced art scene, so he rented a studio in Brooklyn's

Richard Serra

One of the twentieth-century's most influential sculptors, Richard Serra was born in San Francisco, California, in 1939. According to the artist, an event he witnessed at the age of four—the launching of a ship from the shipyard where his father worked—left him in awe of steel, and most of his artistic career has been dedicated to exploring the structural possibilities of the metal. Serra's steel sculptures can be massive and imposing, but like a ship on the sea, there is also undeniable grace and balance at work.

Serra began working with steel in the late 1960s. He created slabs, cubes, and other simple forms, and along with other artists exhibiting similar work, he was labeled by the critics as a "minimalist." Minimalism puzzled some viewers, but the movement and the intellectual arguments proffered by its leading figures influenced later artists, notably Martin Puryear and **Maya Lin** (1949–; see entry in volume 2 and update in volume 3), creator of the Vietnam Veterans Memorial in Washington, D.C.

Serra's work set off a controversy when his *Tilted Arc* (1981) was installed in Federal Plaza in New York City. The large steel sculpture upset people because it blocked their passage across

Richard Serra. Photograph, © Richard Schulman. Reproduced by permission of the Corbis Corporation.

the plaza, and following a heated legal battle that involved the sensitive issue of freedom of expression, the work was finally removed from its site and destroyed in 1989. The controversy just enhanced Serra's fame, and he has continued to produce large steel works such as *Torqued Ellipses* (1997), a work composed of graceful curves.

Williamsburg neighborhood. Puryear's work from the 1970s shows him building on all of the traditions that had formed his tastes, including African and Scandinavian woodworking and American minimalist sculpture. *Cedar Lodge* (1977) is an 18-foot-tall hut made of cedar, fir, and rawhide. *Self* (1978) is a painted wood sculpture resembling a huge thumb. An important work from this period is the two-part *Box and Pole* (1977), which had to be installed outdoors because the pole is one hundred feet high.

Works and teaches in Chicago

In 1978, a fire destroyed Puryear's Brooklyn studio, and soon afterwards he took a teaching position at the art school of the University of Illinois's Chicago campus. Spurred by either the destruction of the fire or the change in environment, his work went in new directions. He became intrigued by yurts, simple and portable huts built by the inhabitants of Central Asia, and built sculptures that borrowed structural elements from yurts. Historical figures also fascinated him, especially black explorer Matthew Henson (1866–1955) and James Beckwourth (1798–1867), an ex-slave who lived among Native Americans for much his life. *Equation for Jim Beckwourth* (1980) is a seventy-foot-long wall sculpture made of wood, rawhide, and other materials. Puryear has said the work honors its namesake's talent for adapting to new situations—a talent the restless artist has had to cultivate.

In 1982, Puryear designed and executed *Bodark Arc,* the most ambitious work of his career. He created it for the Nathan Manilow Sculpture Park, several acres in Illinois dedicated to contemporary sculpture. *Bodark Arc* consists of low arches, a footbridge, chairs, and other pieces, all made of wood, leading the visitor in a semicircular path through swamps, over ponds, and across a prairie. The work is so large that somebody walking along its path cannot really understand what the whole structure looks like. Only from high in the air can the shape of the work be comprehended, although this perspective misses out on the experience of walking through it. The artist purposely made the work so that it can be experienced in more than one way.

Puryear thrived in the 1980s, both as an artist, and as a teacher at the University of Illinois, where he inspired young artists to experiment with form and to draw on whatever historical or philosophical sources interested them. His work went in two different directions during this decade, and these two types of work have continued to typify his artistic output. Inspired by nature, Puryear created *Cask Cascade* and *Old Mole* in 1985; both resemble birds' heads, or perhaps the hoods that falconers make for hawks. These works use wood in a way that connects the material to its natural origins. Almost like trees, they seem to grow up from the floor of the museum or gallery. Alternatively, Puryear has also been drawn toward humankind's invention of tools. An untitled sculpture from 1987 seems like it might be an enormous handle from a shovel or other implement, although it might also be seen as a mouse or as two abstract forms—a ring and part of a cone. Part of the enjoyment of his work is trying to figure out how to identify a form; the artist seems to have fun keeping people guessing. The wall sculpture *Greed's Trophy* (1984) and the long floor piece *Lever #2* (1988–89) resemble traps for wild animals.

Achieves wider recognition

Puryear's challenging yet easily enjoyable sculpture has made him one of the most respected artists of his generation, and 1989 was an especially good year for him professionally. He was the recipient of the John D. and Catherine T. MacArthur Foundation Fellowship Award, also known as a "genius grant," and he received the grand prize for best artist at the São Paulo Bienal, Brazil. Two years later, the Art Institute of Chicago honored Puryear with a retrospective. Appropriately, it was the art museum in the city that had been Puryear's home for some of the most important years of his career that bestowed this honor upon him. By the time the show went up, however, Puryear had relocated once again, this time to upstate New York, to a house and studio he designed in collaboration with architect John Vinci. In 1999, California's Getty Center, an institution known for exhibiting artwork from past centuries, commissioned Puryear to make an outdoor sculpture. He responded with the towering but delicate *That Profile;* the work stands majestically against the southern California landscape.

For More Information

Books

Benezra, Neal. *Martin Puryear.* Chicago: The Art Institute of Chicago, 1991.

Warren, Lynne. *Art in Chicago: 1945–1995.* Chicago: Museum of Contemporary Art, 1996.

Web Sites

"Martin Puryear." *African-American History Through the Arts.* [Online] Available http://cghs.dade.k12.fl.us/african-american/twentieth_century/puryear.htm (last accessed on July 3, 2001).

"Martin Puryear." *Donald Young Gallery.* [Online] Available http://www.donaldyoung.com/martin_puryear_index.html (last accessed on July 3, 2001).

"Martin Puryear." *The Getty Center.* [Online] Available http://www.getty.edu/art/collections/bio/a3781-1.html (last accessed on July 3, 2001).

Raphael

Born April 6, 1483
Urbino, Italy

Died April 6, 1520
Rome, Italy

Italian painter and architect

A master of the Italian High Renaissance, Raphael is widely considered one of the most popular and influential painters of an era that included such artists as Leonardo da Vinci (1452–1519; see entry in volume 2) and Michelangelo (1475–1564; see entry in volume 2). Raphael lived to be only thirty-seven years old, but in his short lifetime he rose to great prominence and created some of the world's most significant and beautiful works of art. His designs can still be found decorating several rooms of the Vatican, and his tapestries hang beneath Michelangelo's painted ceiling in Rome's Sistine Chapel. Characterized by his superb technical ability and a serene, spiritual outlook, Raphael's paintings show the influence of the masters who taught him, as well as the development of his own personal style.

During the High Renaissance, a period beginning around 1500 and lasting about twenty-five years, the vigorous intellectual and artistic developments that had begun in Italy a century earlier reached their peak. The word "renaissance," which means "rebirth," describes a return to the achievements and values of the classical era—the period in which the ancient civilizations of Greece and Rome flourished. This revival, along with a new appreciation for the strength of human reasoning and the worth of the individual (not just society as a whole) characterized what is known as the humanistic philosophy that took hold during the Renaissance. The artistic achievements of the High Renaissance included the practice of narrative art, or using art to tell a story and interpret events; the accurate portrayal of the human body as a means of expressing emotion or a state of mind; and the careful composition of the elements of a painting to create a harmonious sense of balance. Michelangelo, Leonardo da Vinci, and Raphael (the youngest of the three) were masters of these aspects of artistic representation.

A cultured childhood

Born Raffaello Sanzio in Urbino, Italy, the artist came to be known simply as Raphael (pronounced RAF-ee-el), or Raphael of Urbino. His mother, Magia di Battista Ciarla, died when Raphael was eight years old. His father, Giovanni Santi (another version of Sanzio), was a moderately successful artist and poet. He began training his son in the techniques of painting when Raphael was a very young boy, and he introduced the child to a world of great refinement and culture. Before Raphael's birth, Urbino had been ruled by Duke Federigo da Montefeltro (1422–1482), a military figure who had a passionate love for the arts. He filled his court with some of the great artists of the day, establishing Urbino as a vibrant cultural center. Giovanni Santi worked as a painter for the ruling Montefeltro family, and the young Raphael no doubt was exposed to the stimulation of that court. When Raphael was eleven years old, his father died. Biographers differ about how he spent the next several years, with some saying he was raised by relatives and others suggesting that he was apprenticed to a painter in Urbino, Timoteo Viti.

◀ *Self-Portrait*. Painting by Raphael. Photograph reproduced by permission of the Corbis Corporation.

By the time he was seventeen years old, Raphael had gained recognition for his burgeoning talent, and was described by some as a master. Sometime around 1500, he went to Perugia, a community in the region of Umbria, Italy, to study with and assist painter Pietro Perugino (1445–c. 1523). Raphael learned quickly, absorbing Perugino's lessons so completely that many of Raphael's works from this time are almost indistinguishable from those of his instructor. From Perugino, Raphael learned about creating a balanced, organized composition. His drawing of faces, particularly the serene, idealized beauty of the women he painted, also owes a debt to Perugino.

Raphael's *The Marriage of the Virgin,* depicting the wedding of Mary and Joseph, displays the influence of Perugino but also shows Raphael's emerging artistic individuality. The painting closely resembles a work of the same name painted by Perugino; the people in the two paintings look alike, they occupy similar positions in the foreground, and they wear comparable clothing. Both works take place in a courtyard, with a large, domed temple in the background. But while Perugino's work is rigidly balanced and symmetrical, Raphael's composition is a bit more informal; he achieves the same sense of harmony and balance but in a more relaxed way. Raphael's figures appear more natural and lifelike, their expressions more tender and real. The temple in the background is more complicated in Raphael's painting, revealing his interest in architecture. This painting also shows Raphael's command of perspective, the technique of showing depth, distance, and the relationship of objects to each other on a flat surface. The viewer realizes that the temple in the background is much larger than the people in the foreground, yet their actual size in the painting is almost the same. One way Raphael created this optical illusion was to make the people standing close to the temple much smaller than those placed in the foreground.

Onward and upward

After a few years studying under Perugino, Raphael began to look elsewhere to further his artistic education. He moved to Florence in about 1504, perhaps drawn there by

reports of the artistic heights being reached in that city by Michelangelo and Leonardo da Vinci. (It was around this time that Michelangelo had finished one of his masterworks, the towering statue *David,* and Leonardo was causing a sensation with his *Mona Lisa.*) Raphael studied the works of those great masters, and his paintings from this period—and indeed for the rest of his life—reveal their tremendous influence.

Madonna of the Chair (ca. 1513). *Painting by Raphael. Galleria Palatina, Florence. Photograph, © Francis G. Mayer. Reproduced by permission of the Corbis Corporation.*

297 | Raphael

The Virgin Mary in Renaissance Art

While Mary's name does not appear in the New Testament of the Christian Bible more than a few times, her importance—particularly in the Catholic religion—as a figure of motherly love, forgiveness, and divine grace is profound. For more than a thousand years, artists have been inspired by these qualities and have attempted to capture them in their works. The life of the Virgin Mary, mother of Jesus Christ, has inspired many of the world's most cherished works of art.

Artistic depictions of the Virgin Mary reached a peak of creative excellence during the Renaissance era (approximately 1400–1600) in Europe. The greatest artists of the period (ranking among the greatest artists of all time) portrayed various pivotal events in the life of Mary. These events include her marriage to Joseph; the Annunciation, or the moment when the angel Gabriel announced to Mary that she would conceive Jesus Christ; the birth of Jesus, also called the Nativity; scenes of Mary in a field with the baby Jesus playing nearby; Mary's grief-stricken response to the Crucifixion of Jesus Christ, images known by the description Pietà; and the Assumption, or the moment when Mary was lifted into heaven—body and soul—at the end of her Earthly life.

Among the best-known works of High Renaissance painter Raphael are his *The Marriage of the Virgin* (1504) and *La Belle Jardinière* (1507–8), a peaceful countryside scene of the Virgin Mary and the baby Jesus. Leonardo da Vinci, with his tender depiction of Mary and Jesus in *The Virgin of the Rocks* (two versions, 1483 and 1503–6), influenced all who followed. Michelangelo (1475–1564) portrayed the touching scene of Mary holding Jesus' dead body on her lap in his famous *Pietà* (1498–99).

Raphael's most notable works from this period include a series of Madonna and Child paintings, idyllic works showing the Virgin Mary with the infant Jesus Christ. The Madonna is one of the most widely chosen subjects for artists the world over, and Raphael's Madonna paintings are the standard by which others are measured. Raphael's own standard for these works, however, was Leonardo's *Virgin of the Rocks,* painted twice, first in 1483. Here, the Madonna and baby Jesus were posed in the shape of a triangle, and in such works as *La Belle Jardinière* and *Madonna of the Goldfinch,* Raphael used a similar composition. Raphael was also deeply impressed by Leonardo's skill in depicting the interplay between light and shadow, a technique known as *chiaroscuro* (pronounced key-AR-uh-SKEEUR-oh). Another technique of Leonardo's, called *sfumato* (pronounced sfoh-MAH-toe) also influenced Raphael. *Sfumato* involves using a soft, subtle blending of color tones instead of hard lines to define the outline of a person or an object. Raphael's paintings bear the mark of Leonardo, but the young painter was able to incorporate the influences of the master without simply imitating him. Raphael's numerous paintings of the Madonna and Child display his own unique gifts; they radiate an unmatched peacefulness, with Mary portrayed as a tender, ideally beautiful woman.

All roads lead to Rome

After only a few years in Florence, Raphael's fame had spread to Rome. The artist's work had come to the attention of Pope Julius II (1443–1513), one of the greatest art patrons of the Renaissance era. Julius had earlier commissioned Michelangelo to paint the ceiling of the Sistine Chapel, and in 1508 he enlisted Raphael to further realize his plans to beautify Rome. Wishing to update the Vatican in the style of the Renaissance, Julius hired Raphael to paint several rooms, known collectively as the *stanze,* in the part of the Vatican where the pope lived and worked. The resulting works not only established Raphael's reputation in Rome during his lifetime but also cemented his legacy as one of the world's most important painters. He spent the next several years painting the frescoes, works painted directly onto freshly plastered walls, completing some of the great masterpieces of his career.

The first room Raphael completed, the Stanza della Segnatura, contains one of his most famous paintings, the *School of Athens.* Depicting some of the greatest thinkers of ancient Greece and Rome, *School of Athens* in many ways typifies High Renaissance art. The painting is filled with people in various stages of motion—some walking, some sprawling on stairs, some standing in groups, engaged in heated discussion. The layout is complicated yet harmonious and balanced. Each

group of people seems interconnected with the others, and all lead the eye to the two men in the center of the painting: ancient Greek philosophers Plato (c. 428–c. 348 B.C.) and Aristotle (384–322 B.C.). Other major figures from ancient Greece include mathematicians Euclid (lived c. 300 B.C.) and Pythagoras (c. 580–c. 500 B.C.) and philosopher Heracleitus (c. 540–c. 480 B.C.). The inclusion of such people, as well as the style of architecture of the building in which they are shown, point to a deep admiration of classical civilization. The fluid, athletic movements of the figures reveal the close attention paid to anatomy by Renaissance painters. And Raphael's mastering of perspective is not just a technical achievement; it also conveys an impression of the continuity of learning and knowledge throughout time. Raphael found a way to pay tribute to the great artists of his own time, connecting them to the brilliant minds of the past: The man representing Plato is painted to resemble Leonardo da Vinci. The face of Euclid is said to be modeled on Renaissance architect Donato Bramante (1444–1514), while Heracleitus may have been based on Michelangelo. And tucked into the bottom right corner of the painting, looking out at the viewer, is Raphael himself.

The second room containing Raphael's frescoes, called Stanza d'Eliodoro, depicts the power of the Catholic church through scenes of miraculous events. By the time he had begun working on these frescoes in 1512, Raphael had become one of the most well-known artists in Rome. After the death of Julius II, Raphael enjoyed the patronage of Julius's successor, Pope Leo X (1475–1521). Raphael was in such demand that he had to employ dozens of assistants to help in the execution of his larger works. The remaining two rooms in the Vatican that he had been commissioned to paint—the Stanza dell'Incendio and Sala di Constantino—were completed in large part by these assistants, with Raphael providing only designs, instruction, and some painting. In 1514, Raphael was hired to assist Bramante, architect of the new St. Peter's Basilica in Rome. After Bramante's death later that year, Raphael took over, adding his own touches to Bramante's design for the church.

"The prince of painters"

In addition to being a gifted artist, Raphael was handsome and charming. Unlike some of his more temperamental and unstable fellow artists, Raphael intended to please his patrons and followed through on promised projects. The combination of such qualities made Raphael one of the busiest artists in Rome. Among other projects, Raphael became one of the most important portrait artists in the city, painting several of Rome's most powerful citizens. At the same time, Raphael became involved in archaeological undertakings, charged by the pope with the task of uncovering and preserving relics from ancient history. The pope also hired Raphael to decorate the walls of the Sistine Chapel with a series of woven tapestries. Raphael created a set of ten "cartoons," which are full-scale paintings copied by weavers. These designs, depicting events in the lives of Jesus Christ's apostles, reveal Raphael's ability to use images to tell a story. The expressiveness and emotional depth of the tapestries influenced artists for generations to come.

Part of Raphael's continuous development and innovations as an artist involved further study of the works of Leonardo da Vinci and Michelangelo. Many art historians speculate that Raphael snuck into the Sistine Chapel to view Michelangelo's ceiling paintings before they were unveiled to the public. He was so struck by the powerful, dramatic athleticism of Michelangelo's figures that he immediately began incorporating some of the great artist's principles into his own paintings. His masterpiece *The Triumph of Galatea* shows his fascination with bodies in motion. The goddess Galatea occupies the center of the painting; her dramatic red cloak is draped over her twisting body. She is surrounded by sons and daughters of sea gods, all of whom are shown in various stages of motion. The men in particular are larger than life, extremely athletic and muscular. All of the figures, like those in Michelangelo's paintings, seem to have the full dimensions of a sculpture rather than the flatness of a painting. In this, as in most of his works, Raphael revived what he considered the glorious spirit of the ancient Greek and Roman civilizations.

In 1519, Giulio de' Medici, a cousin of Pope Leo X, commissioned Raphael to paint a scene from the life of Jesus Christ to be placed at the altar of a cathedral in France. While working on this painting, *The Transfiguration,* in 1520, Raphael became ill. He died on his thirty-seventh birthday, which that year fell on Good Friday, the day commemorating the death of Jesus Christ. Raphael, described by admirers as "the prince of painters," was widely mourned.

For More Information

Books

Barter, James. "Raphael the Stylist." *Artists of the Renaissance.* San Diego, CA: Lucent Books, 1999.

Beck, James H. *Raphael* (Masters of Art series). New York: Harry N. Abrams, Inc., 1994.

Jones, Roger, and Nicholas Penny. *Raphael.* New Haven, CT: Yale University Press, 1987.

Mühlberger, Richard. *What Makes a Raphael a Raphael?* New York: The Metropolitan Museum of Art, 1993.

Vasari, Giorgio. *Lives of the Artists,* Vol. 1: A Selection Translated by George Bell. London: Penguin Books, 1987.

Web Sites

"Raffaello Sanzio (Raphael)." *Uffizi.* [Online] Available http://www.televisual.net/uffizi/raphael.html (last accessed on July 3, 2001).

"Raphael." *CGFA.* [Online] Available http://sunsite.dk/cgfa/raphael/ (last accessed on July 3, 2001).

"Raphael (Raffaello Sanzio)." *Mark Harden's Artchive.* [Online] Available http://www.artchive.com/artchive/R/raphael.html (last accessed on July 3, 2000).

Rembrandt van Rijn

Born July 15, 1606
Leiden, Netherlands

Died October 4, 1669
Amsterdam, Netherlands

Dutch painter and etcher

UPDATE

Ranked among the world's finest painters, Rembrandt lived and worked during a period of tremendous prosperity and artistic achievement in the Netherlands. His fame began early—by age 25, he had established a reputation as a masterful portrait painter in the Dutch city of Amsterdam. In addition to portraits (of himself as well as others), Rembrandt van Rijn, who signed his works with just his first name, is known for his paintings of Biblical scenes and for hundreds of etchings used for printmaking. Admired for his brilliant technique and rich colors, Rembrandt made frequent use of *chiaroscuro* (pronounced key-AR-uh-SKEEUR-oh), a method of depicting the contrasts of light and shadow to lend a full, realistic appearance to the flat surface of a painting. His greatest accomplishment, however, was conveying the personality and emotional depth of his subjects. As described by Henry Adams in *Smithsonian* magazine, "His paintings . . . seem to peer into the inner soul of his subjects." **(See original entry on Rembrandt in volume 2.)**

Much of the impact of Rembrandt's paintings comes from his skillful depiction of facial expressions. Rembrandt did not select conventionally beautiful people to paint, preferring instead a face filled with character and feeling. He often embellished his subjects with props from his collection: furs, velvet drapes, golden chains, and exotic hats. Rembrandt's rich, thick brushstrokes gave an almost three-dimensional quality to the lush fabrics he painted. In one of his most famous works, *Aristotle Contemplating a Bust of Homer,* Rembrandt depicts Greek philosopher Aristotle (384–322 B.C.) thoughtfully examining a statue of Greek poet Homer (lived c. 8th century B.C.). Both figures are bathed in a warm light, and Aristotle's thick gold chain and silk robe seem to glow. In dozens of self-portraits, Rembrandt documents changes in his own style, fortune, and outlook throughout his life, from the confidence of the 1630s works to the weariness of his final self-portrait in the year of his death. Perhaps Rembrandt's best-known work is an action-filled painting of a group of soldiers called *The Militia Company of Captain Frans Banning Cocq,* better known as *Night Watch* (1642). The level of activity and animation in this group portrait differs from similar types of works painted by Rembrandt's contemporaries—most group portraits of the time showed rows of people sitting perfectly still—and the initial reaction to *Night Watch* was mixed. Over time, however, the painting has been widely recognized as a masterwork.

Questions of authenticity

An admired and respected painter, Rembrandt attracted numerous students who wished to study at his side and learn the techniques of the master. It was a common workshop practice at the time for students to copy the works of the instructor, and for the instructor to sign his name to some of his students' works. In some cases, historians suspect that Rembrandt's students worked directly on paintings begun by Rembrandt. These practices have led to a great deal of confusion in modern times over which paintings are Rembrandts, and which ones are exceptionally good copies. In the centuries since Rembrandt's

◀ **Self-Portrait (1640). National Gallery, London.** *Reproduced by permission of the Corbis Corporation.*

Rembrandt van Rijn

death, there have also been numerous convincing forgeries of his works, further complicating the attempt to determine authenticity.

Beginning in the 1960s, Rembrandt scholars took a closer look at the hundreds of paintings attributed to the Dutch master and concluded that many of them were not actually painted by Rembrandt. Before 1965, it was thought that around 630 Rembrandt paintings existed; since then, various scholars have trimmed that number to about 300. Museums all over the world were compelled to reexamine their priceless Rembrandts, in some cases concluding that the works they owned were nothing more than well-executed imitations. In 1995, the prestigious Metropolitan Museum of Art in New York staged an elaborate exhibition called "Rembrandt/Not Rembrandt." This exhibition, unusual because major museums are generally reluctant to acknowledge that any works in their collection might not be authentic, explained what scholars had done to assess Rembrandt's paintings and showed the difference between a real Rembrandt and a phony one. Scholars have assessed a painting's authenticity by examining technique and style as well as by using modern scientific methods like X-ray photography, which shows the structure, or various layers, of a painting, and microscopic paint analysis, which can indicate the time period when the paint was manufactured.

In 1998, X-ray technology helped scholars determine that a painting long believed to be a Rembrandt, *Self-Portrait with Gorget,* was in fact a copy. The painting, which hung in the Mauritshuis museum in the Hague, a city in the Netherlands, was virtually identical to one in a museum in Nuremberg, Germany. X rays of the Mauritshuis painting showed that the artist had drawn an outline before applying paint. Scholars knew that Rembrandt did not draw outlines for his paintings, so they concluded that this painting was a copy. Another important work thought to be a Rembrandt but recently reevaluated is *The Holy Family in the Evening.* In this case, it was not scientific analysis but a judgment about the painter's style that convinced the experts. The style of the painting, which shows the infant Jesus Christ, the Virgin Mary, and Joseph bathed in a warm light, seemed similar in many ways to that of Rembrandt. But while Rembrandt was a master at capturing emotion, the strongly sentimental tone of this work seemed uncharacteristic of Rembrandt's more restrained style. Researchers determined that the painting had probably been done in Rembrandt's studio by an accomplished student. Dozens of other works that may or

◀ Aristotle Contemplating a Bust of Homer *(1653). Painting by Rembrandt. Oil on canvas. 143.5 x 136.5 cm* Metropolitan Museum of Art, New York. Photograph, © Geoffrey Clements. Reproduced by permission of the Corbis Corporation.

Masterworks

1632	*The Anatomy Lesson of Dr. Nicolaes Tulp*
c. 1635	*Rembrandt and Saskia*
1636	*Danaë*
1638	*Samson Threatening His Father-in-Law*
1642	*The Militia Company of Captain Frans Banning Cocq,* or *The Night Watch*
1650	*Christ Healing the Sick (Hundred Guilder Print)*
1654	*Aristotle Contemplating a Bust of Homer*
	Bathsheba
	Jan Six
1658	*Self-Portrait*
1662	*Syndics of the Drapers' Guild*
c. 1664	*The Jewish Bride*

may not be Rembrandts await attribution while various researchers argue stylistic and scientific points. Scholars have debated for decades over the authorship of Rembrandt's works, and they will continue to do so for decades to come.

For More Information

Booksand Periodicals

Adams, Henry. "Rembrandt or Not Rembrandt?" *Smithsonian* 26 (December 1995): p. 82.

Clark, Kenneth. *An Introduction to Rembrandt.* New York: Harper & Row, 1978.

Mühlberger, Richard. *What Makes a Rembrandt a Rembrandt?* New York: Viking, 1993.

Wetering, Ernst van de. *Rembrandt: The Painter at Work.* Berkeley, CA: University of California Press, 2000.

Web Sites

"Rembrandt." *Culture Pavilion.* [Online] Available http://parallel.park.org/ Netherlands/pavilions/culture/rembrandt/ (last accessed on July 3, 2001).

"Rembrandt." *WebMuseum, Paris.* [Online] Available http://www.ibiblio.org/wm/paint/ auth/rembrandt/ (last accessed on July 3, 2001).

"Rembrandt van Rijn." *Mark Harden's Artchive.* [Online] Available http://www.artchive.com/artchive/R/rembrandt.html (last accessed on July 3, 2001).

Frederic Remington

Born October 4, 1861
Canton, New York
Died December 26, 1909
Ridgefield, Connecticut

American painter and sculptor

F rederic Remington built a reputation as an artist who brought the "Old West" to life. In magazine illustrations, paintings, and sculptures, he showed cowboys and Indians riding horses and in battle, driving stagecoaches across treacherous landscapes, and shooting it out in saloons. Throughout his career, Remington built upon and enlarged the myth of the Old West, showing life not as it really was in America in the nineteenth century but as it was imagined in the literature of the day. Remington flourished before the dawn of the motion pictures, but his mythmaking is at the foundation of the "Western" movie genre.

Remington's contribution to American mythology is profound, but for many commentators and historians there are problems with his version of American history. In particular, he celebrated rather than mourned the tragic fate of Indians, or Native Americans, choosing to represent them as uncivilized, savage warriors. Remington's view of the world, as seen in his

> *"I knew the wild riders and the vacant land were about to vanish forever . . . and the more I considered the subject, the bigger the forever loomed."*

▲ *Frederic Remington.*
Reproduced by permission of the Corbis Corporation.

writings, was prejudiced and narrow-minded, reflecting to some extent the attitudes that were not uncommon in the era in which he lived. Nevertheless, his artistic skill was considerable, and he excelled in both painting and sculpture at capturing the magnificent spectacle of a horse at full gallop.

A love of horses and art

Frederic Sackrider Remington was the only child of journalist and newspaper owner Seth Pierre Remington and Clara B. Sackrider. Shortly after he was born, his father fought for the North in the Civil War (1861–65), serving as captain in Louisiana, Mississippi, and Arkansas. This experience served as the basis for many stories relayed from father to son in the years to come. The two of them shared a passion for horses, attending races and fairs together.

Horses were among Remington's favorite subjects when he sketched. Between 1876 and 1878, when he attended the Highland Military Academy in Worcester, Massachusetts, he entertained his classmates with caricatures of the teachers. It was on the basis of his artistic skill (and not his academic performance) that he gained admission to Yale's School of Fine Arts in 1878. A fine athlete, Remington participated in boxing, wrestling, and football, playing in a famous game between Yale and Princeton in 1879. Sports proved more satisfying than time in the studio, which was more regimented and academic than he would have preferred.

When Remington's father died unexpectedly in February 1880, he quit school to take an office job working for the New York governor in Albany. He spent most of his time daydreaming about the Old West, recalling stories that his father had told him about more thrilling times and landscapes. When Remington turned twenty-one years old, he followed one of his college friends to Kansas and started a small ranch. He kept horses and sheep, performing all the necessary chores with enthusiasm and saving enough time in the evenings to do watercolors and pen-and-ink studies. The experience was also profitable, and by 1884 he had sold the ranch and returned to

New York State to marry Eva Caten, whom he always called "Missie." The couple briefly settled in Kansas City, Missouri, but soon relocated to Brooklyn, New York.

Finds work in New York

Remington signed up for classes at the Art Students League in preparation for a career as a magazine illustrator. (The technology did not yet exist for printing photographs in magazines, so illustrators were much in demand.) He knew that this work paid more than that of a painter. *Harper's Weekly* was one of the most popular magazines of the era, and it consequently paid the most. He decided, however, that before he could approach the editors, he had to travel more. Popular magazines were full of stories that glorified life in the western part of the United States, and Remington wanted to see these regions for himself. He journeyed to Arizona, sketching canyons, military outposts, and, of course, horses. The high point of his trip was witnessing the final days of the famous campaign against the Apache Indians. The battle ended in 1886, when Colonel George Crook (1829–1890) captured Geronimo (1829–1909), the great Apache chief.

Harper's printed some wood engravings based on Remington's watercolors of Crook's campaign, and a magazine called *Outing* published more work on the same subject. As his illustrating career blossomed, magazines would pay for him to travel to destinations such as Texas and the Canadian Rockies. Remington was overweight and, by his own admission, could not have endured the trials of the frontier, but his career gave him the opportunity to take part in what he saw as an exciting and adventurous life. He took a camera along with him and photographed landscapes and faces that captivated him, building up an archive of images for future artwork.

The pictures Remington gave the magazines reflected his tastes in art, which tended toward detailed and bloody scenes from the Franco-Prussian War and the Napoleonic Wars, and in particular, the work of French painter Jean-Louis-Ernest Meissonier (pronounced mess-ahn-YAY, 1815–1891). At the time, Meissonier was much respected in America, though the name has fallen out of prominence. Remington appreciated his technical skill and the vitality of this work, qualities he tried to import into his own artistic efforts. In February 1888, Remington illustrated a series of articles written by future president Theodore Roosevelt (1858–1919) for *Century Magazine.* These articles were later published in book form as *Ranch Life and the Hunting Trail.* Remington's images went perfectly with ideals about the American frontier promoted by the increasingly popular Roosevelt.

Illustration versus art

As Remington's reputation as an illustrator grew, so did his ambition to achieve success as a fine artist. Illustrators had to base their work on articles printed in magazines, but artists had the freedom to choose any subject that pleased them. Furthermore, artists enjoyed greater prestige and, if very successful, greater financial rewards. He began exhibiting his work in the Brooklyn Arts Club and other venues in 1889 and found the sales and reviews encouraging.

He continued accepting assignments from *Harper's* and other magazines, staying on the road four months of the year or more to gather material for illustrations. In 1892, he left American soil for the first time, traveling to Russia to chronicle the life of soldiers in this foreign land. He visited Germany, France, and England on the way back, and at some point traveled to North Africa, but he greatly preferred the landscape and comforts of the United States.

Part of breaking away from illustration involved creating images that made statements on their own, with no particular connection to the stories they accompanied in magazines. In the final decade of the nineteenth century, Remington created many such images, including the quiet, wintry *Fall of the Cowboy* (1895) and *Captured* (1899). For Remington, *Fall of the Cowboy* represented the decline of not just cowboys but the white race. It was his feeling that other races were spoiling America. In *Captured,* a bare-chested, hatless American sol-

dier is bound hand and foot, while four Indians—three seated, one standing in a heroic pose—watch over him. In many ways, *Captured* is a typical Remington: usually the white men have all the dignity, while the Indians are full of savagery.

Gives sculpture a try

In 1895, Remington produced his first sculpture, *The Bronco Buster.* A cowboy holds on to a bucking bronco with one hand, while the other hand draws back to give the animal another taste of the switch. Altogether, Remington produced twenty-two different sculptures, all of them variations on the horse-and-rider theme. Some of them show Native Americans in the saddle, while others show the horses descending perilous slopes. *Coming through the Rye,* perhaps his most famous sculpture, shows four cowboys riding horses and firing pistols into the air.

Fight for the Waterhole (1903). Painting by Frederic Remington. Oil on canvas. *Museum of Fine Arts, Houston, Texas. Hogg Brothers Collection, Gift of Miss Ima Hogg. Reproduced by permission of Bridgeman Art Library.*

Thousands of reproductions of these sculptures have been produced, thanks to what is known as "lost-wax casting." With this process, the sculptor starts by making a clay model, from which a plaster cast is made. The plaster cast is used to create a hollow mold commonly made of glue or gelatin. In the next step, melted wax is brushed into the interior of the glue mold. Finally, molten bronze is poured into the mold, remelting the wax, which drains away. The outer mold is then broken, leaving a bronze sculpture that retains much of the detail of the original clay model, if the complex process is followed properly. The problem, say experts, is that many of the Remington bronzes currently in circulation are of an inferior quality. It is likely that the artist would disavow responsibility for much of the work that now carries his name.

Continues into the twentieth century

Like many readers of the magazines he worked for, Remington felt a great deal of nostalgia for the heyday of cowboys. This era was over before his career started, and by the time the twentieth century began, it seemed more distant than ever. He may have recognized that much of the nostalgia was based on exaggeration and, sometimes, outright fiction, but in a changing world, the myth of the Old West felt reassuring.

Remington made his most stirring and powerful artworks in the final years of his life. In 1903, he began an association with *Collier's* magazine, which had pioneered a way of including color in its pages. Furthermore, the magazine gave him the freedom to make artworks on any subject he chose. His first work for *Collier's* was *Fight for the Waterhole,* a tense scene of American soldiers on the lookout for Indian warriors. *Apache Medicine Song* (1908) shows seven men gathered around a campfire. Although their poses suggest cavemen or apes—a fact that, according to some critics, reveals the artist's prejudice—the picture nevertheless has a gentle quality. Remington was only forty-eight years old when he died of appendicitis. Roosevelt, whose exploits out West and during the Spanish-American War of 1898 the artist had commemorated, said of Remington, "He has portrayed a most characteristic and yet vanishing type of American life."

For More Information

Books

Hassrick, Peter H. *Frederic Remington.* Forth Worth, TX: Amon Carter Museum, 1973.

Nemerov, Alexander. *Frederic Remington & Turn-of-the-Century America.* New Haven, CT: Yale University Press, 1995.

Shapiro, Michael Edward. *Cast and Recast: The Sculpture of Frederic Remington.* Washington, DC: The Smithsonian Institution Press, 1981.

Web Sites

"Frederic Remington." *Artcyclopedia.* [Online] Available http://www.artcyclopedia.com/artists/remington_frederic.html (last accessed on July 3, 2001).

Frederic Remington Art Museum. [Online] Available http://www.remington-museum.org/ (last accessed on July 3, 2001).

Masterworks

1895	*The Fall of the Cowboy*
1899	*Captured*
	The Charge of the Rough Riders
1902	*Coming through the Rye*
1903	*Fight for the Waterhole*

Faith Ringgold

Born October 8, 1930
New York, New York

American painter and quiltmaker

UPDATE

". . . I want to make a connection with people, to communicate my concerns, which are expressed in my work. I want to in some way touch their lives and give them reinforcement and inspiration for their own problems."

F aith Ringgold, an artist, teacher, and social activist, has been creating memorable works of art reflecting the African American experience for more than thirty years. Particularly concerned with the limitations society has placed on black women, Ringgold has, through her artworks and her involvement with various organizations, worked to celebrate her culture and improve the representation of black artists in the mainstream art community. **(See original entry on Ringgold in volume 2.)**

Ringgold began her career creating politically themed oil paintings in the 1960s. One such work, *U.S. Postage Stamp Commemorating the Advent of Black Power* (1967), protested against the poor state of race relations between blacks and whites. In the 1970s, Ringgold began incorporating traditional African techniques into her works, using embroidery, beads, and pieces of cloth. She produced several works with colorful, woven frames (rather than the traditional wood or metal) and sewed life-sized masks and cloth sculptures. With the change in medium came a shift in content: Ringgold left behind the angry social statements of her 1960s works, deciding instead to celebrate the rich cultural heritage of African Americans.

Echoes of Harlem

In 1980, Ringgold began working with her mother, a dressmaker and fashion designer, on a quilt called *Echoes of Harlem,* which featured the faces of many people Ringgold had known as a child. Harlem, a mostly black neighborhood in New York City, was home to the Harlem Renaissance, a flowering of creative and intellectual activity in the 1920s and 1930s. The neighborhood was home to many black writers, artists, and social activists when Ringgold was growing up. After her mother's death in 1981, Ringgold decided to continue creating quilts, and by 1984 she had begun incorporating text into her works. The resulting "story quilts," with the words surrounding a central image painted on fabric, depict scenes derived from Ringgold's imagination as well as from memories of stories relatives had told her. Her series of story quilts called "Women on a Bridge" includes one of her best-known works, *Tar Beach,* which tells the story of a young girl who uses dreams and her imagination to fly away from her poverty-stricken life.

Spreading her wings

After a trip to Paris in 1991, Ringgold created a series of story quilts called "The French Collection." This series, completed in 1997, is a fantasy of a young African American woman named Willa Marie Simone who goes to Paris in the 1920s and becomes a famous artist. Ringgold creates her own version of art history with these quilts—a history that prominently features female and African American artists in a field dominated by white males. Ringgold followed up "The French Collection" with a series called "The American Collection," which features Willa Marie's daughter Marlena. Again depicting a world that is more ideal than real, Ringgold tells the story of Marlena's rise to fame as an artist in America. The series

The Flag Is Bleeding #1
(1990). Illustration by Faith
Ringgold. © Fine Arts
Museum of Long Island.
Reproduced by
permission of Bernice
Steinbaum Gallery.

addresses Marlena's reactions to the lingering effects of slavery, which Ringgold describes as "an unfinished issue that is still affecting us." She explores slavery in depth in her most recent series, "Coming to Jones Road: Part One," which celebrates African American slaves' escape to freedom through the Underground Railroad in the years before the American Civil War (1861–65). Ringgold's status as an important African American artist brought her several commissions for public art projects in the 1990s. She created *Flying Home: Harlem Heroes and Heroines* (1996), two 25-foot murals that were installed in New York's 125th Street subway station. She also produced a story quilt called *The Crown Heights Children's Story Quilt,* which portrays the many different cultures that settled the Crown Heights neighborhood in Brooklyn, New York.

In the early 1990s, Ringgold began expanding her story quilts into children's books. Her book *Tar Beach* (1991) became a bestseller and earned the prestigious Caldecott Honor Book Award as well as the Coretta Scott King Illustrator Award in 1992. That book became the basis for numerous other projects, including two board books for very young children, *Counting to Tar Beach* and *Cassie's Colorful Day* (both 2000). *Tar Beach,* narrated by pop and rhythm-and-blues singer Natalie Cole (1950–), was included in an Emmy-winning HBO special that aired in December 1999 and featured the voices of celebrities reading much-loved children's stories. In addition to *Tar Beach,* Ringgold wrote several other acclaimed children's books throughout the 1990s as well as her autobiography, *We Flew Over the Bridge* (1995). The reference to flying in the title of her autobiography reflects her belief that everyone can realize their dreams. "In everything I make," Ringgold explains, "I'm trying to say that anyone can fly. You just have to believe you can do it."

Masterworks

1967	*U.S. Postage Stamp Commemorating the Advent of Black Power* (painting)
1983	*Who's Afraid of Aunt Jemima?* (quilt)
1988	*Tar Beach* (quilt)
1991–97	"The French Collection" (quilts)
1996	*Flying Home: Harlem Heroes and Heroines* (mural)
1997	"The American Collection" (quilts)
	The Flag Is Bleeding #2 (quilt)

For More Information

Books

Farrington, Lisa E. *Art on Fire: The Politics of Race & Sex in the Paintings of Faith Ringgold.* New York: Millennium Fine Arts, 1999.

Ringgold, Faith. *Talking to Faith Ringgold.* New York: Crown Publishers, 1995.

Ringgold, Faith, ed. *Dancing at the Louvre: Faith Ringgold's French Collection and Other Story Quilts.* Berkeley: University of California Press, 1998.

Web Sites

"About Faith Ringgold." *Scholastic.* [Online] Available http://teacher.scholastic.com/authorsandbooks/authors/ringgold/bio.htm (last accessed on July 3, 2001).

"Faith Ringgold." *Department of Visual Arts, University of California San Diego.* [Online] Available http://visarts.ucsd.edu/faculty/fringgol.htm (last accessed on July 3, 2001).

Micucci, Dana. "A U.S. Artist's Homage to French Muses." *International Herald Tribune.* [Online] Available http://62.172.206.162/IHT/SR/102498/sr102498h.html (last accessed on May 31, 2001).

Ringgold, Faith. *anyIcanfly.* [Online] Available http:// www.art-incontext.org/artist/ringgold/ (last accessed on July 3, 2001).

Norman Rockwell

Born February 3, 1894
New York, New York

Died November 8, 1978
Stockbridge, Massachusetts

American illustrator and artist

Norman Rockwell is one of the most famous—and most beloved—American artists. Best known as the illustrator of several hundred covers of the *Saturday Evening Post* magazine, Rockwell created charming, old-fashioned portrayals of an idealized small-town America. Whether portraying kids playing baseball, a young couple at a soda shop after the prom, or soldiers returning home from war, Rockwell was able to tap into people's hopes for the future and fond memories of the past. But in spite of his widespread popularity among the American public, Rockwell has been dismissed by many art historians and critics for being overly sentimental. His detractors suggest that his works lack complexity and subtlety. His supporters, however, argue that the value of his artwork is that it appeals to people of all walks of life and that it represents the powerful attraction of an ideal America—where all citizens are kind, honest, moral, and hard-working. Rockwell's art is undoubtably American, and celebrates the nation's most uplifting aspects.

> *"I have always wanted everybody to like my work. I could never be satisfied with just the approval of the critics . . . or a small group of kindred souls."*

▲ *Norman Rockwell.*
Courtesy of the Library of Congress.

Success comes early

Norman Perceval Rockwell was born in a bedroom of his family's apartment building in New York in 1894. His father, J. Waring Rockwell, was a businessman and amateur artist. Norman inherited artistic talent from his mother's side of the family as well: Nancy Hill Rockwell's father (Norman's grandfather) was an artist, though an unsuccessful one. Rockwell began drawing as a boy, discovering early that he had a talent for accurately capturing an image with a few, quick pencil strokes. A skinny, awkward boy, Rockwell longed for the athletic ability of his brother, Jarvis, but had to content himself with his drawing skills. He later wrote of his art: "Because it was all I had I began to make it my whole life. I drew all the time. Gradually my narrow shoulders, long neck, and pigeon toes became less important to me." Once he began high school, Rockwell started to take art classes in his spare time. By the middle of his sophomore year, in 1909, he knew he wanted to devote more time to his art education. Surprising his family, Rockwell quit school to enroll in the National Academy of Design. He only stayed there a year, however, eventually rejecting what he called the school's "stiff and scholarly" atmosphere. In 1910, he enrolled at the Art Students League, where his teachers instructed him not only in the finer points of drawing and painting, but also in how to become a professional illustrator.

While still studying at the Art Students League, Rockwell was hired to illustrate a series of children's books called *Tell Me Why.* That project led to work illustrating *Boys' Life,* the magazine for the Boy Scouts. Within a year, at age nineteen, Rockwell was promoted from occasional illustrator to art director of the magazine. His working relationship with the Boy Scouts would continue until the end of his life—he provided illustrations for their calendar nearly every year for half a century. By now a full-time illustrator of graphic art (art created to sell a product or to complement text), Rockwell found jobs with numerous magazines and publishers of children's books. His early success came fairly easily, but he soon longed for more. He wanted to illustrate adult magazines, and he set his sights at the top: the *Saturday Evening Post.*

Graphic Art vs. Fine Art

Graphic art includes advertisements, posters, book and magazine illustrations, cartoons, and web site design. Occasionally referred to as "low art"—as opposed to "high," or fine art such as paintings and sculptures found in museums—graphic art is generally relegated to second-class status. There are those who prefer to divide graphic art and fine art into black-and-white categories: Graphic art is created to sell a product, promote an ideology, or, in the case of illustration, to complement text. Fine art, on the other hand, is created purely as a thing of beauty, or as an expression of an artist's emotions or ideas. Graphic art is designed to appeal to the widest possible audience, while fine art need only please the artist.

In reality, such categories are not so easily defined. Sometimes graphic art is elevated to the level of fine art, and sometimes fine art is appropriated for commercial purposes. Norman Rockwell's paintings, many of which were created as magazine covers for the *Saturday Evening Post,* have been dismissed by some critics as too sentimental to be considered high art. His works, however, have been displayed in some of the most prestigious museums in the United States and have sold for sums of nearly one million dollars. Fine artist **Aleksandr Rodchenko** (1891–1956; see entry in volume 4) created political posters and advertising campaigns that fall squarely in the realm of graphic design. His innovative and bold designs, however, influenced graphic and fine artists alike. Pop artist Andy Warhol (c. 1928–1987; see entry in volume 2) blurred the lines between commercial and fine art with his paintings of Campbell's soup cans and his three-dimensional replicas of Brillo pad boxes.

Belgian artist **René Magritte** (1898–1967; see entry in volume 4) started his career in commercial art, grew to detest advertising, and became a highly respected fine artist. In spite of his distaste for the field, dozens of advertisers later imitated Magritte paintings to sell televisions, insurance, cars, and more. And one of the most respected artworks of all time, *Mona Lisa* (1503 –05) by Leonardo da Vinci (1452–1519; see entry in volume 2), has been used in countless advertisements.

The *Saturday Evening Post*

In 1916, the *Saturday Evening Post* was the most widely read magazine in the United States and one of the most prestigious for illustrators. Rockwell became determined to illustrate the cover of this major magazine. He took several sample covers to the *Post*'s offices in Philadelphia, and the magazine's art director and its publisher liked his work so well that they immediately hired him to paint several covers. Rockwell's first *Saturday Evening Post* cover appeared on May 20, 1916—the beginning of a career-making relationship for the artist. Titled *Mother's Day Out,* this work shows a dressed-up boy pushing a baby in a carriage while two passing kids, dressed for a baseball game, tease him that he must babysit instead of playing ball. Throughout his career, Rockwell repeatedly explored the joys and humiliations of childhood. Other common themes include young romance, relationships between children and the adults they encounter, and the simple pleasures of small-town life. Regardless of the subject matter, Rockwell's illustrations are characterized by their ability to tell a story and to evoke feelings of amusement, sympathy, or nostalgia.

In the same year Rockwell was hired for his first *Saturday Evening Post* cover, he married a schoolteacher named Irene O'Connor. Shortly after his marriage to Irene, Rockwell enlisted in the U.S. Navy. Although he served in the military during World War I (1914–18), he never had combat duty. Once his artistic abilities were discovered by his superiors, Rockwell was assigned to draw cartoons for a naval newspaper. In his spare time, he painted portraits of navy personnel and continued doing illustrations and covers for a variety of magazines. Throughout the 1920s, Rockwell became increasingly successful and famous. He became the primary cover artist for the *Post,* his covers appearing on the weekly magazine more often than those of any other illustrator. For the issues that featured a Rockwell illustration on the cover, the *Post* printed thousands of extra copies to meet increased demand. Among his most enduring covers from that period was *Doctor and Doll* (1929), which depicts a country doctor holding his stethoscope to the chest of a little girl's doll. While Rockwell is generally identified with the *Post,* he did illustrations for several other national magazines as well, including *Life* and *Collier's.* He also supplemented his income by illustrating advertisements for steel companies, life insurance firms, and such foods as Jell-O gelatin and Orange Crush soda pop. Rockwell's income rose steadily, he enjoyed a busy social life, and he made frequent trips to Europe and elsewhere. The decade ended on a sour note, however: Rockwell's marriage to Irene ended in 1929.

Soon after his divorce from Irene was final, Rockwell married another schoolteacher, a woman named Mary Rhodes Barstow. Together they had three sons, and their marriage lasted for nearly thirty years, until Mary's death in 1959. In the early 1930s, the happiness in Rockwell's personal life was offset by a period of insecurity about his work. His many travels exposed him to artistic innovations taking place throughout the world, and Rockwell struggled to find a more modern style. His new direction was not appreciated by his editors at the *Post,* however, and after months of experimentation, Rockwell returned to his familiar style: using realistic, almost photographic, details to capture an amusing moment or tell a touching story. As his prominence grew, Rockwell was hired for a variety of prestigious projects, including the illustrations for the classic Mark Twain (1835–1910) books *The Adventures of Tom Sawyer* and *The Adventures of Huckleberry Finn,* and the painting of several U.S. presidents' portraits. In spite of his popular and commercial success, however, Rockwell was generally either ignored or insulted by art critics. While fans described his gift as an ability to touch their emotions, critics said Rockwell was corny and manipulative—instead of challenging people's intellects, he took the easier route to their hearts.

The "Four Freedoms"

Nearly a year before the United States entered World War II (1939–45), President Franklin Delano Roosevelt (1882– 1945) gave a speech in which he outlined four basic rights, or freedoms, for which the Allied powers were fighting the war. Inspired by that speech and driven to express his patriotism and contribute to the war effort, Rockwell began working on four paintings that would depict the freedoms described by Roosevelt. After struggling to create powerful images that could illustrate such lofty ideas, Rockwell finally discovered the most effective way to reach people. As he later wrote, "I'll express the ideas in simple everyday scenes. . . . Take them out of the noble language of the proclamation and put them in terms everybody can understand."

OURS...to fight for

FREEDOM FROM WANT

The resulting paintings, enormously popular with the American public, are considered by many to be his greatest works. In *Freedom of Speech,* Rockwell painted a handsome, sincere man standing up to speak at a town meeting. *Freedom from Fear* shows parents in the simple act of tucking their sleeping children into bed. A large, cheerful family sits down to a bountiful Thanksgiving dinner in *Freedom from Want.* And

Freedom of Worship shows a close-up view of several people, of different ages and from different backgrounds, with their hands folded in prayer. Rockwell's simple images touched the emotions of many Americans. Originally published in the *Saturday Evening Post,* the paintings prompted millions of requests from people wanting reprints. Eventually the paintings toured the country to raise money for war bonds, which are essentially loans made to the government by citizens to finance a war. The "Four Freedoms" paintings helped raise over $130 million for the U.S. government.

Goodbye to the *Post*

In 1961, two years after the death of his wife Mary, Rockwell married Molly Punderson. Two years later, after nearly fifty years of creating their covers and story illustrations, Rockwell ended his relationship with the *Saturday Evening Post.* Rockwell's liberal political views, though not overtly expressed in his artwork, had become harder and harder to reconcile with the magazine's conservative slant. He began working for *Look* magazine, experiencing a dramatic shift in the kinds of pictures he wanted to paint. As he wrote, "For 47 years, I portrayed the best of all possible worlds—grandfathers, puppy dogs—things like that. That kind of stuff is dead now, and I think it's about time." Rockwell felt a new energy and sense of purpose as he set out to capture the social issues of the time in his works. *The Problem We All Live With,* one of his best-known paintings, shows a little African American girl being escorted to school by federal marshals. The wall behind the girl shows splattered tomatoes thrown by onlookers as well as racist graffiti. Court-ordered school integration, which forced formerly all-white schools to admit black students, aroused anger among those who felt the races should remain separate. Some of the black students, therefore, required the protection of law enforcement officials to get to school safely.

Until he reached the point where his aging mind and body made painting difficult, Rockwell continued to capture slices of American life on canvas. His painting of the *Apollo 11* astronauts

Masterworks

1921	*No Swimming*
1929	*Doctor and Doll*
1943	The "Four Freedoms" series
1951	*Saying Grace*
1957	*After the Prom*
1958	*The Runaway*
1960	*Triple Self-Portrait*
1961	*Golden Rule*
1964	*The Problem We All Live With*

just before the first moon landing in 1969 prompted some to note that Rockwell's career had spanned a vast segment of American history, from the early days of automobiles and airplanes to spaceships landing on the moon. Although he stopped painting in the mid-1970s, Rockwell's popularity and success continued to grow. He received the Presidential Medal of Freedom—the highest award given in the United States during peacetime—in 1977, and the Norman Rockwell Museum in his hometown of Stockbridge, Massachusetts, still attracts visitors from all over the country. While many art critics continue to dismiss Rockwell as a mere illustrator rather than a fine artist, others have praised his exceptional technique and his ability to paint pictures that tell a story with humor, sensitivity, and grace.

For More Information

Books

Durrett, Deanne. *The Importance of Norman Rockwell.* San Diego, CA: Lucent Books, 1997.

Gherman, Beverly. *Norman Rockwell: Storyteller with a Brush.* New York: Atheneum Books for Young Readers, 2000.

Hennessey, Maureen Hart, and Anne Knutson. *Norman Rockwell: Pictures for the American People.* New York: Harry N. Abrams, Inc., 1999.

Web Sites

The Norman Rockwell Museum at Stockbridge. [Online] Available http://www.nrm.org/home.html (last accessed on May 31, 2001).

Aleksandr Rodchenko

Born December 5, 1891
Saint Petersburg, Russia
Died December 3, 1956
Moscow, U.S.S.R.

Russian designer, photographer,
painter, and sculptor

One of the most important Russian artists of the twentieth century, Aleksandr Rodchenko was an innovator in every art form that he practiced. In addition to painting, he designed bold and intriguing political posters, took photographs from unusual angles, produced collages that combined photographs and newsprint into unusual compositions, and built amusing sculptures out of wood and industrial materials. In all of these pursuits, Rodchenko showed a love of geometric forms and the rhythms of modern life. He was a key figure in the artistic movement known as constructivism and exerted an influence on painters and designers not just in Russia, but throughout Europe and America, too.

Rodchenko's homeland underwent tremendous political change during his lifetime. The Communists in Russia incited a revolution in 1917, and the country became known as the Union of Soviet Socialist Republics (U.S.S.R.). Rodchenko and other artists, poets, and intellectuals of this period struggled to cope with political changes by creating work that broke

"Live in the present, bow down to the living idols, creators, geniuses, inventors! Give the living the chance to create calmly—support them! Give life to the living and death to the dead."

new ground without provoking the wrath of the Soviet government. Rodchenko survived the rotating cast of Soviet leaders and their unpredictable policies, but ultimately, according to commentators, political forces beyond the artist's control defeated his ambitions. Writer Luc Sante has described Rodchenko's career as a "textbook example of the seduction and betrayal of the Russian Revolution."

Humble beginnings

Thirty years before Aleksandr Rodchenko was born, the serfs (the Russian social class whose lives were not much better than slaves) gained freedom to live wherever they wanted and to own land. The artist's father, Mikhail Mikhailovich Rodchenko, was the son of a serf who found work as a theater caretaker. His mother, Ol'ga Evokimovna Paltusova, worked as a washerwoman. As a young child, Rodchenko was fond of the circus and the harbors and canals of Saint Petersburg. Art was not among his interests, despite the presence in Saint Petersburg of the Hermitage, one of the world's great art museums. Art became a passion later, after the Rodchenkos moved to the eastern city of Kazan around 1905.

Although the city was far away from the cultural centers of Europe, the Kazan School of the Arts exposed Rodchenko to developments in art at the start of the twentieth century. A friendship with a local art collector led him to the discovery of Russian art as well as French painters Henri Matisse (1869–1954; see entry in volume 2) and Paul Gauguin (1848–1903; see entry in volume 1), whose experiments in form and subject matter were revolutionizing the art of painting. He also loved literature, including the novels of Fyodor Dostoyevsky (pronounced dos-tuh-YEF-skee) and the plays of Oscar Wilde (1854–1900). (Rodchenko would later design costumes for some of Wilde's plays.) Aubrey Beardsley (1872–1898), an English artist who created dreamlike line drawings illustrating Wilde's works, became an early influence on Rodchenko. He also met Varvara Stepanova in Kazan, and she became his lifelong companion and frequent collaborator. Their daughter, Varvara Rodchenko, was born in 1925.

Discovers modern art

In February 1914, Rodchenko attended a lecture and performance promoting the thinking of the newly formed Russian futurists, a group of artists and writers who wanted Russian art and literature to reflect the latest trends from Europe. Poet Vladimir Mayakovski (1893–1930) especially impressed Rodchenko, and a long association began between the two men. Rodchenko's work began reflecting the work of European artists, including Italian painter and sculptor Umberto Boccioni (1882–1916) and French painter Fernand Léger (1881–1955). Across Europe, experimental artists were attempting to create forms inspired by machines rather than by nature; consequently, sharp angles and thick lines replaced delicate curves and gentle shading. Rodchenko's painting *The Dancer* (1915), in which the human figure of the title is barely recognizable through the fragmented shapes, reflects this ambition.

In keeping with these modern tendencies, Rodchenko's next step was to eliminate the suggestion of human figures altogether and to present geometric forms that did not represent anything that existed in nature. With such work, known as "pure abstraction," artists demonstrate the visual interest of simple triangles, circles, and so forth. Many of Rodchenko's paintings from 1918 are simply titled *Bespredmetnaia kompozitsiia,* which translates as *Non-Objective Composition.* By this time, he was living in Moscow and debating the purpose and direction of art with other painters and sculptors.

Political events influence his world

In February of 1917, the last czar (an inherited title similar to king) was forced to step down, and in October of that year, Vladimir Lenin (1870–1924) and the Bolshevik political party took control of Russia. The Bolsheviks practiced Communism, an economic and social theory in which the state holds all the wealth and property and distributes them according to the needs of the citizens. Rodchenko was one of a group of artists sympathetic to Communism and therefore well positioned to have their ideas about art accepted by the new government and, in

"We created a new understanding of beauty and enlarged the concept of art."

this way, spread to a broader audience. Along with painter Kazimir Malevich (1878–1935) and sculptor and monument-builder Vladimir Tatlin (1885–1953), Rodchenko seized this opportunity despite occasional confusion over whether the artists' ideals truly matched those of the Bolsheviks.

Rodchenko, Malevich, and Tatlin each had their own distinct artistic attitudes and ambitions. For Malevich, art was a spiritual activity, and the extremely simple forms in paintings such as *Black Square on White* (1913) and *White on White* (1918) reflect his beliefs about the universe. (Rodchenko responded with a series of black-on-black paintings.) Tatlin's most significant project was his *Monument to the Third International* (1920), a design for a spiraling structure, intended as headquarters for the Communist party, that would have been the tallest in the world if it had been built. A few years earlier, his artworks made of combinations of wood, rope, metal, and other materials helped to kick off the constructivist movement.

This movement originated as a reaction against the limitations of easel painting—that is, paintings on canvas made to be hung on the wall. The "constructions" of the constructivists featured the geometric forms of modern painting, but like sculptures they existed in three dimensions. Starting around 1919, Rodchenko led a branch of the movement called "productivism," which advocated the production of objects in factory-like settings. His *Spatial Construction no. 12,* formed of plywood circles of various sizes, is the only one of his works from this period that still exists. Critics note that Rodchenko succeeded in creating a complex three-dimensional object out of simple two-dimensional shapes.

Tries other art forms

Whereas most art did not serve any function, Rodchenko envisioned purposeful art, such as lamps, that embodied the artistic principles of the constructivists. Such ideals were linked to the Communists and their mistrust of the wealthy and their art collections. The artist believed strongly in the principles and policies of the Communist party, and his loyalty led to

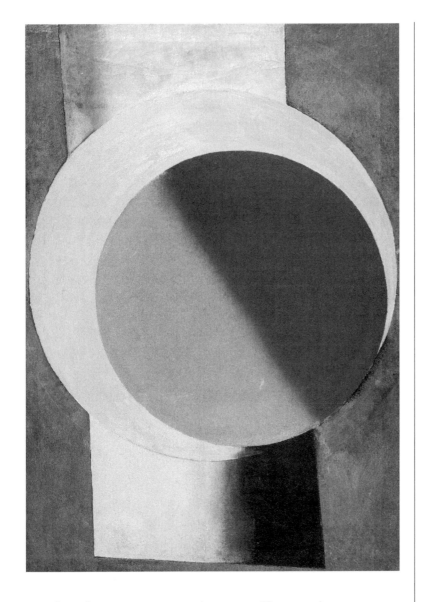

a series of government appointments. He served as secretary and then director of an institute devoted to ensuring that artists produced work that was in line with Communist principles.

In 1921, at a group exhibition in Moscow titled *5 x 5 = 25*, Rodchenko exhibited a purely red painting, a purely blue painting, and a purely yellow painting and announced that the art of painting was over. He turned to graphic design, a field that included posters and advertising images. Many artists before

Masterworks

c. 1920	*Spatial Construction no. 12*
1923	Advertising posters for the state airline Dobrolet
1928–30	*Assembling for a Demonstration*
1928	*At the Telephone*

and since have considered graphic design beneath them, but he saw it as a chance to reach more people and to persuade them of Communism's benefits. The work Rodchenko created during the 1920s is sometimes criticized as propaganda, which means it is more political than artistic; it is nevertheless stunning in its inventive use of color and shape.

Among Rodchenko's most powerful graphic work are his posters, enamel pins, and other designs for the state-run airline, Dobrolet. Incorporating a simple drawing of a propeller plane and creatively lettered slogans, this work inspired confidence in the relatively new prospect of traveling by air. His collaboration with Mayakovski, which began in 1923, produced billboards advertising cigarettes, bread, and other goods produced by the state. It is odd to think of a great poet and an innovative artist working on such projects, but they believed that by helping the government, they were helping the people and furthering goals that they placed ahead of the standard definitions of beauty. Whatever their intentions, the bold and energetic graphics do, in fact, have a visual appeal that goes beyond their immediate purposes as advertising and have influenced not just graphic designers but fine artists as well. American painter Stuart Davis (1894–1964; see entry in volume 1) is just one figure who seems to have benefited from Rodchenko's example.

Rodchenko's graphic design work led to an interest in photography, and he added the camera to his collection of tools for creating art that was revolutionary both visually and politically. In 1926, he photographed Mayakovski for the cover of the poet's book *Conversation with the Finance Inspector about Poetry;* the design featured propeller planes circling a globe superimposed (by collage) on Mayakovski's bald head. He delved into the field, absorbing influences from France and Germany, the centers of photographic experimentation at the time. The most recognizable characteristic of his pictures was the dramatic camera angles he favored. For a 1925 series titled "The Building on Miasnitkaia Street," he stood on the sidewalk a few feet from the building and pointed his camera almost straight up in the air. The resulting images are extremely foreshortened views of the building, which means that the parts that are close seem much bigger than the parts that are far away. *Na telefone* (*At the Telephone,* 1928) employs a similar strategy for showing a newspaper worker talking on a phone that is mounted to the wall. Rodchenko took this picture from almost directly above the worker's head.

Confusion over art and politics

After Russia became the U.S.S.R., Lenin ruled the country with an iron hand, but after he died in 1924, his harsh tendencies were surpassed by his successor, Joseph Stalin (1879–1953). Rodchenko stayed loyal to the government even when it developed into a brutal and merciless force. His loyalty guaranteed him continued governmental work, but as art became less important to the Soviets, Rodchenko no longer had as much of an impact on his country. By the 1940s, he was discouraged and disillusioned by the way history had turned out. "I'm absolutely unneeded, whether I work or not, whether I live or not," he wrote in his diary in 1945. In the years since his death in 1956, the artist's reputation is inevitably tangled up with his political views. Some historians view him as an innocent "pawn" of history, while others, recognizing the impossibility of ignoring his politics and his association with repressive dictatorships, struggle to reconcile his position as a propagandist for the Soviet government with his artistic innovations.

For More Information

Books

Dabrowski, Magdalena, Leah Dickerman, and Peter Galassi. *Aleksandr Rodchenko.* New York: The Museum of Modern Art, 1998.

Margolin, Victor. *The Struggle for Utopia: Rodchenko, Lissitzky, Moholy-Nagy*. Chicago: University of Chicago Press, 1997.

Tupitsyn, Margarita. *The Soviet Photograph: 1924–1937*. New Haven, CT: Yale University Press, 1996.

Web Sites

"Aleksandr Rodchenko." *The Museum of Modern Art*. [Online] Available http://www.moma.org/exhibitions/rodchenko/ (last accessed on July 3, 2001).

Sante, Luc. "After the Revolution." *Slate.com*. [Online] Available http://slate.msn.com/Art/98-07-15/Art.asp (last accessed on July 3, 2001).

Schjeldahl, Peter."The Revolutionary." *Artnet.com*. [Online] Available http://www.artnet.com/Magazine/features/schjeldahl/schjeldahl7-16-98.asp (last accessed on July 3, 2001).

Mark Rothko

Born September 25, 1903
Dvinsk, Russia
Died February 25, 1970
New York, New York

American painter

M ark Rothko is famous for his paintings of the 1950s and 1960s—large rectangles of one color overlaid with one or more rectangular fields of another color. Despite their simplicity, these works are regarded as fascinating experiments in how colors interact and powerful expressions of the times in which they were produced. One of the leading figures of abstract expressionism, Rothko differs stylistically from **Jackson Pollock** (1912–1956; see entry in volume 2 and update in volume 4) and **Willem de Kooning** (1904–1997; see entry in volume 3) and other painters of this school; while they splattered paint and applied violent brushstrokes, he treated colors in a way that makes them seem to float in mid-air. Abstract expressionism is a movement in American art associated with the energetic application of paint on the canvas; it is concerned with the expression of emotion rather than the realistic portrayal of figures or landscapes, for example.

"I'm interested only in expressing basic human emotions— tragedy, ecstasy, doom, and so on."

▲ *Mark Rothko. Reproduced by permission of AP/Wide World Photos, Inc.*

Many viewers experience a sense of calmness when viewing a Rothko painting in person. The artist's life, however was anything but calm. Born in Russia, he moved to America at the age of ten and worked hard to make ends meet. During his brief period at Yale University and throughout his painting career, Rothko had a long string of personal conflicts and constantly doubted the choices he made. When, after a series of health problems including bouts with depression, he committed suicide in 1970, his paintings seemed to take on a new significance and continue to be seen as evidence of his internal strife.

From Russia to America

Marcus Rothkovich (also spelled Rothkowitz) was born in the town of Dvinsk (now Daugavpils), then part of Russia but now part of Latvia. His father, Jacob Rothkovich, was a Lithuanian-born pharmacist, and his mother, Kate Goldin Rothkovich, was Prussian. Both parents came from Orthodox Jewish backgrounds, and Marcus was pressured to attend *cheder* (pronounced KAY-der), a school where religious studies predominated. The youngest of four children, he resisted his religious education, complaining it was unfair that his sister and brothers did not also have to go.

The family emigrated to Portland, Oregon, in 1913 to improve its financial prospects and to escape anti-Semitism (prejudice against Jews). Tragically, Jacob Rothkovich died of colon cancer the following year. This event was especially traumatic for Marcus, eleven years old and struggling to learn English and to grow accustomed to life in America. The Portland school system placed immigrant children of all ages in first grade, a humiliating experience for a boy his age. He had to work selling newspapers on the street, though he was neither strong nor competitive enough to profit at this job. His only pleasures were reading and going on long hikes, "in front of the endless space of the landscape of Oregon lying covered by wintry snows," as he later described it.

Marcus Rothkovich (he did not change his name to Rothko until 1940) surmounted his early academic difficulties and proved himself a skilled writer and debater. Politics interested him, and he thought about a career fighting on behalf of labor unions (organizations of workers bargaining with employers for improved wages and benefits). In 1921, he and two friends from Portland were accepted for admission into Yale University in New Haven, Connecticut. His family expected him to become a lawyer.

Decides to become an artist

Whether because of anti-Semitism or political intolerance, Rothkovich found Yale unwelcoming. He developed a mistrust of students from wealthy backgrounds and showed little interest in his classes. After two years of college, he decided to move to New York City. While his friends pursued careers as doctors and lawyers, he made vague plans for a life in either theater or music; he played the mandolin.

"Then one day," as Rothko later told a writer from *Time* magazine, "I happened to wander into an art class. All the students were sketching this nude model—and right away I decided that was the life for me." He began his art education under the direction of Arshile Gorky (born Vosdanik Adoian; 1904–1948) and Max Weber (1881–1961), both of whom encouraged their student in the direction of abstraction. Abstract art, first practiced in Europe early in the twentieth century, involves creating shapes and forms that may be inspired by, but do not closely resemble, how things appear in the real world.

An artist's life in the early 1930s, during the economic hard times known as the Great Depression, was full of hardship and discouragement. Rothkovich met and married Edith Sachar in November 1932, and the two led an impoverished life while he threw himself into painting. He formed a friendship with American painter Milton Avery (1893–1965), and through him became involved in a circle of artists with similar interests. American artists of the 1930s and 1940s were determined to find a style all their own rather than imitating the work of the Europeans. Rothkovich personally worked through many styles in his quest to find, in his words, "a pictorial equivalent

Untitled painting (pink, creme, mauve, and blue) by Mark Rothko (1946–47). Tate Gallery, London/Art Resource, NY. Reproduced by permission.

for man's new knowledge and consciousness of his more complex inner self."

Transforms his life and work

In 1940, Marcus Rothkovich became Mark Rothko, a name easier to remember and less likely to advertise his Jewishness. That was not the only change in his life during the early 1940s. His marriage to Sachar ended, and he soon married Mary Alice ("Mell") Beistle, a commercial artist almost twenty years younger than Rothko. More important to Rothko's development as an artist was his friendship with Clyfford Still (1904–1980), an American painter whose ideas about abstract art as a life-or-death struggle exerted a powerful influence on Rothko and his circle.

In January 1945, Rothko had a solo show at the Art of this Century Gallery, owned by Peggy Guggenheim (1898–1979), a powerful booster of American art at a time when the more prestigious Museum of Modern Art was mainly showing European work. The exhibition enhanced Rothko's reputation in the art world but resulted in only three sales. Guggenheim herself purchased *Slow Swirl at the Edge of the Sea,* an abstract work in which rounded shapes seem to dance on a brown-gray landscape. The shapes seem to suggest two figures side by side, possibly one male and one female, though critics have debated which is which.

The presence of figures in a landscape, even as abstract as they are in *Slow Swirl,* meant that Rothko's art had not yet achieved complete abstraction, a state where nothing on the canvas refers to anything at all in the real world. With Still's encouragement, Rothko moved further in this direction, and by the late 1940s, Rothko's paintings no longer showed figures, landscapes, or anything else recognizable. They were "about" color, shape, and the artist's psychological state. In a related development, poetic titles such as *Slow Swirl* and *The Omen of the Eagle* gave way to titles such as *Red on Maroon* and *Number 1, 1949,* which were designed to focus the viewer on the work and nothing else. The process of eliminating subject matter from his work was painful and difficult, especially for an artist like Rothko who craved popularity. The reaction to these more abstract paintings was lukewarm, until recognition came in the form of cash—a thousand dollars from the Rockefeller family for *Number 1.* The Rockefellers, who had made their money in the oil industry, were prominent supporters of the arts, notably the Museum of Modern Art. Rothko's career seemed to be looking up.

"There is no such thing as good painting about nothing."

Mark Rothko, on what he called "a widely accepted notion among painters that it does not matter what one paints, as long as it is well painted."

Masterworks

1944	*Slow Swirl at the Edge of the Sea*
1949	*Number 1, 1949*
1951	*Number 12, 1951*
1964–67	The Rothko Chapel
1969	*Black on Grey*

Finds his style

After a number of personal and philosophical squabbles, Rothko's friendship with Still was over by 1950. The lessons he learned during their association, however, continued to dictate the course of his artistic development. Rothko's signature style—rectangles of color that seem to float in space—came about through intensive experimentation and endless discussions with fellow artists about the relationship between the viewer and the painting. He achieved striking color effects through the application of several layers of thin, watery paint. By sticking to the same style, Rothko was able to explore it in all its variety. In addition, having a signature style helped gallery visitors and potential buyers recognize his work. They would look at a picture and immediately know it was a Rothko.

New York in the 1950s is now regarded as one of the most vital scenes in the history of art. Sometimes called the New York school and sometimes abstract expressionists, the painters of this movement included Rothko, Jackson Pollock, Willem de Kooning, and a handful of others. Celebrated within the art world, they were the subject of harsh reviews and mocking dismissals in newspapers and magazines read by the general public. As time went on, these painters led the way in changing people's ideas about what art was supposed to look like. Although Rothko shared many of their ideals, he tended to prefer solitude and did not join the other artists when they congregated. He did, however, share with Pollock and de Kooning a tendency to drink too much. In addition, he suffered from depression and periodically found himself unable to paint.

Success and setbacks

By then end of the 1950s, Rothko's career was finally taking off. When architect and arts patron Philip Johnson (1906–

) designed a skyscraper for the Seagram Corporation, Rothko was commissioned to paint murals for its restaurant, the Four Seasons. Harvard University invited him to paint murals for a campus dining room, and the artist accepted, if only to settle a score with Harvard's rival, Yale. In 1961, the Museum of Modern Art organized a retrospective that eventually traveled to London, Amsterdam, Rome, and Paris. These hallmarks of success, however, often rubbed the artist the wrong way. Accustomed to confrontation throughout his life, he found himself getting into conflicts even with people who wanted to celebrate his achievements. For example, he changed his mind and decided not to give Seagram the murals he had created for its restaurant; he said the wealthy people eating there would fail to appreciate his artistic aims.

In 1965, the de Menil family commissioned Rothko to create a set of murals for a Catholic chapel in Houston, Texas. The Rothko Chapel, as it is now known, is considered one of his masterpieces. The large, dark murals inside seem to encourage spirituality, though critics point out that neither the de Menil's Catholicism nor Rothko's Judaism is the focus of that spirituality. Rather, it is a temple to Rothko and his genius.

Rothko had an aneurysm (a problem with circulation in the brain) in 1968, and thereafter he experienced a number of health problems, all of which were aggravated by smoking, drinking, and overeating. He fought constantly with his wife and his oldest friends and resolved never to paint again. Rothko committed suicide on a winter day in 1970. Even then, the problems generated by a life of conflicts did not go away; a legal battle over his last will and testament continued well into the following decade.

For More Information

Books

Ashton, Dore. *About Rothko.* New York: Da Capo, 1996.

Breslin, James E. B. *Mark Rothko: A Biography.* Chicago: The University of Chicago Press, 1993.

Glimcher, Marc. *Mark Rothko: Into an Unknown World.* New York: Crown Books for Young Readers, 1991.

Web Sites

Benfey, Christopher. "Heavenly Rectangles." *Slate.* [Online] http://slate.msn.com/Art/98-05-13/Art.asp (last accessed on May 31, 2001).

"Mark Rothko." *Artcyclopedia.* [Online] http://www. artcyclopedia.com/artists/rothko_mark.html (last accessed on May 31, 2001).

"Mark Rothko." *The National Gallery of Art.* [Online] Available http://www.nga.gov/feature/rothko/ (last accessed on May 31, 2001).

"The Power of Color: Rothko's Legacy." *NewsHour.* [Online] http://www.pbs.org/newshour/bb/entertainment/july-dec98/ rothko_8-5.html (last accessed on May 31, 2001).

Henri Rousseau

Born May 21, 1844
Laval, France
Died September 2, 1910
Paris, France

French painter

K nown as *Le Douanier* (pronounced dwon-YAY), French for "customs officer," Henri Rousseau is best known for such fanciful, richly colored jungle paintings as *The Dream* and *The Hungry Lion*. Largely a self-taught artist, Rousseau ignored many of the confining artistic conventions of his time, painting the world of his imagination without adhering to traditional rules concerning technique, composition, and subject matter. Though his boldly different style was ridiculed at first by critics and other artists, the charm, simplicity, and imaginative power of his paintings eventually won him a devoted following. Classified by many art historians as a primitive or naive painter, meaning an artist who has not had formal training in an art school or by a professional artist, Rousseau represents the transition from the academic world of nineteenth-century art to the revolutionary innovations of modern art in the twentieth century.

"Nothing makes me happier than to contemplate nature and to paint it."

▲ *Henri Rousseau.*
Reproduced by permission of the Corbis Corporation.

Henri Rousseau

The customs officer

Henri Julien Félix Rousseau (pronounced awn-RHEE roo-SO) was born into a family of modest means in Laval, France. He was a mediocre student, excelling in music and art but not much else. As a young man, he worked briefly in an attorney's office. He entered the military after he was caught stealing a small sum of money from his employer. He served one month in prison for the theft in 1863, after which he spent four years in the army. Following the death of his father, Rousseau requested a discharge from the army so he could get a job and support his mother. He moved to Paris and soon began a long career as a civil servant. He worked for the Paris toll office, collecting taxes on shipments of goods that came into the city. In 1869, Rousseau married Clémence Boitard. Together they had seven children, though only two lived through childhood and only one, their daughter Julia, lived past the age of eighteen.

Rousseau's life story is filled with exaggerations and misconceptions, many of which originated with Rousseau himself. During his lifetime, Rousseau encouraged the notion that he had spent time in Mexico as part of his military service, where he lived amidst the lush, tropical vegetation appearing in many of his paintings. In fact, he never left France. His ideas of what a jungle looked like probably came from the descriptions of soldiers who had been stationed in Mexico. He further fed his imagination with pictures from postcards, advertisements, and books of wild beasts. Later, he made numerous visits to the botanical garden at Paris's Museum of Natural History. The Jardin des Plantes ("plant garden") contains species of plants from all over the world and also houses a zoo. Rousseau spent hours at a time there, studying and drawing the plants and animals he observed. A close study of his paintings, however, reveals that his visits to the Jardin des Plantes were more for inspiration than for scientific precision. His renderings of plants and animals are rather fanciful products of his imagination.

Even Rousseau's nickname is rooted in a falsehood. Although he worked for the customs office, his position was several grades lower than that of a customs officer. In any case,

Rousseau somehow became known as Le Douanier, and he did not contradict those who believed he had a more important job than he really did. His job required that he spend long days in a tollbooth, and much of his time was spent observing the scenery around him, admiring the buildings of Paris and watching boats pass on the Seine River. He began painting during his spare time, capturing local settings as well as scenes from his imagination. Even after he began to establish a reputation as an artist, he was still what some people called a "Sunday painter," meaning that he retained a full-time job, painting only on weekends or other days off. In spite of the limited time he initially devoted to painting, Rousseau never considered it a hobby. He had always thought of himself as a full-fledged artist whose circumstances required that he have a steady job to support his family.

First exhibited paintings

It was not until the mid-1880s, when he was around forty years old, that Rousseau exhibited his first paintings. Formally trained and accomplished artists in Paris could exhibit works at the Salon des Artistes Français, known simply as the Salon, which imposed strict rules for painters to follow in terms of style and subject matter. Rousseau's lack of training and unconventional style excluded him from the Salon, but he was able to participate in an alternative exhibit: the annual Salon des Artistes Indépendants, or Salon of Independent Artists. In 1886, he exhibited several paintings there, including *A Carnival Evening*. This painting depicts two people dressed in costumes, emerging from a forest beneath a full moon. The trees, while carefully and literally drawn to show every leafless branch, seem unreal. The moon, while full and shining, does not seem to give off any light. And the costumed people—out of place in this isolated wooded setting—appear to float just above the ground. The overall effect is dreamlike and mysterious. Rousseau did not follow conventional rules about the play of light and shadow, or the blending of colors, but he nonetheless achieved a poetic and dramatic atmosphere.

The reaction to Rousseau's first public exhibition was mixed. Critics and fellow artists did not know exactly what to make of his unusual works. While some expressed admiration for his originality, others ridiculed his naive, childlike approach to art. Far from being discouraged by critics' contempt of his work, Rousseau remained steadfast in his confidence. In fact, he exhibited at the Salon des Artistes Indépendants for many years thereafter. In the midst of his early and tentative success, Rousseau experienced a personal tragedy. His wife, Clémence, died in 1888 after a lengthy illness. Rousseau continued to pursue his art, however, and in 1890 he painted a self-portrait that declared his view of himself as an important and established artist. In *Myself: Portrait-Landscape,* Rousseau depicts himself in a full-length portrait, a composition that, in his day, was usually reserved for important members of society. Complete with a beret, paintbrush, and artist's palette, and surrounded by a Parisian landscape, Rousseau is the very image of a fine French painter. On his palette are inscribed the names of his two great loves: Clémence, and the first name of the woman that would later become his second wife, Joséphine Noury.

A full-time artist

By 1893, Rousseau had been exhibiting at the Salon des Artistes Indépendants for several years. He gradually gained the esteem of critics and other painters, though there were still many who considered him a joke. By this time, Rousseau had developed enough self-assurance to quit his job at the toll booth and devote himself to becoming a professional artist. During these years, he lived in poverty, drawing on a small pension and earning some money from the sale of his paintings. Rousseau also gave lessons in music and painting to supplement his meager income.

In spite of some critics' opinion of him, Rousseau considered himself an artistic genius. He admired and tried to emulate traditional painters, seemingly unaware of how different his style was from theirs. He did not view his paintings as childlike or naive, and he yearned for recognition from the established art world. Instead he found fellowship among the painters and writers of the avant-garde, or experimental, movement in France. It was precisely his departure from the rigid stylistic approach of traditional artists that appealed to these innovators. They admired Rousseau as a pure, innocent, and natural artist whose ideas spring from an imagination free of the inhibiting discipline of formal education. Rousseau's works anticipated the surrealist movement of the early 1900s. The writers and artists who were part of this movement believed that true art should flow freely from the subconscious. They tried to create dreamlike imagery by presenting an altered reality and combining elements that do not ordinarily belong together. Rousseau, while not subscribing to such theories himself, produced art that was in keeping with the surrealist philosophy.

Several of these innovative thinkers befriended Rousseau, helping him gain recognition and credibility among the leading intellectuals in Paris. Alfred Jarry (1873–1907) was one of the first and most important of these friends. Also hailing from the city of Laval, Jarry was a young, nonconformist writer. He believed Rousseau was a gifted, natural artist, and he promoted him in his writings and introduced him to other important figures. Many years later, it would be Jarry who introduced Rousseau to his next champion, French writer Guillaume Apollinaire (1880–1918), and to artists Pablo Picasso (1881–1973; see entry in volume 2) and Robert Delaunay (1885–1941).

One of his most important paintings from this period, *The Sleeping Gypsy* (1897), exemplifies Rousseau's primitive and fascinating style. In the painting, a dark-skinned woman lies sleeping in a barren desert landscape. Beside her on one side are a jug and a stringed instrument, and on the other is a lion, curiously sniffing her but making no move to attack. The woman lies in an unnatural, stiff position, still holding her walking stick. The features of her face are flat, giving no impression of depth. As in most of Rousseau's works, the proportions in this painting are inaccurate: the lion, which appears to be standing very close to the woman, seems much

What Is Primitive Art?

The word *primitivism* has two quite different definitions when applied to works of art. It refers to modern artists' interest in the artworks of tribal cultures—items like masks and sculptures from African countries and elsewhere. Spanish master Pablo Picasso, in such ground-breaking works as *Les Demoiselles d'Avignon* (1907), incorporated features of African masks. Primitivism can also be defined as naive, nonacademic, or folk art—art created by people who have not had formal training and who do not adhere to traditional "rules" about such things as composition, subject matter, and use of color.

Henri Rousseau is the most famous artist to have been given the "naive" label, and in fact the term—as applied to artists—was coined to describe him. Respect and admiration for Rousseau's works came relatively late in his life, but the fact that it came at all encouraged self-taught artists all over the world and awakened the art community to a new category of legitimate art. Many people began to echo the sentiments of Russian painter Wassily Kandinsky (1866–1944; see entry in volume 1), who felt that academic training stifled an artist's innocence and creativity. A person who receives formal artistic training, Kandinsky asserted, "will deliver a 'correct' drawing which is dead." Those who create art without such training, on the other hand, can perhaps better tap into a natural reservoir of talent.

Perhaps the most famous of primitive artists in the United States is Anna Mary Robertson Moses, better known as Grandma Moses (1860–1961). Moses began painting in her seventies, when arthritis in her hands made it too difficult for her to continue with embroidery. She captured quaint country scenes and rural landscapes in such works as *Moving Day on the Farm* (1951) and *Apple Butter Making* (1947). Shortly after some of her works were noticed by an art collector, they were displayed at the Museum of Modern Art and the prestigious Galerie St. Etienne in New York. Grandma Moses quickly achieved international fame for her simple, charming paintings.

smaller than it should be compared to a human. Every line in the painting—from the colorful stripes in the woman's dress to the pointing tale of the lion—is drawn carefully and precisely, yet the overall effect is one of a complete departure from reality. The unreal, poetic atmosphere reflects Rousseau's unique vision.

The Snake Charmer
(1907). Painting by Henri
J. F. Rousseau Musée
d'Orsay, Paris, France.
Photograph reproduced by
permission of Bridgeman
Art Library.

The Dream

Toward the end of his life, in 1905, Rousseau received a measure of the serious recognition he had always known was his due. He was asked to exhibit at the Salon d'Automne, an exhibition including some of the most significant avant-garde artists of the time. Rousseau's painting *The Hungry Lion* was displayed in a position of importance and respect, sharing a room with such painters as Henri Matisse (1869–1954; see entry in volume 2) and André Derain (1880–1954). There were still some who mocked the bold new styles of these painters, who were dubbed by one critic the fauves, or wild animals. Others, however, recognized Rousseau's talent and discussed his works in a positive, serious manner. Important dealers began buying Rousseau's works. Artists such as Delaunay and Picasso and writer Apollinaire became Rousseau's fervent supporters and friends. Picasso bought Rousseau's *Portrait of a Woman,* keeping the painting in his possession until his death. In 1908, Picasso threw a raucous party for Rousseau attended by many intellectuals of the day. Bursting with pride over such

Masterworks

recognition and praise, Rousseau failed to realize that mixed with his friends' genuine affection and regard was a dose of amusement and ridicule. Many regarded Rousseau as a charming oddity; they liked him and his unusual paintings, but they did not always take him seriously.

The final years of Rousseau's career were highlighted by his rich, colorful jungle scenes for which he is most celebrated. In these works, Rousseau creates a fantasy world. He tames the wildness and chaos of the jungle, imposing a carefully composed structure onto the scene. In many of these works, a dramatic, frequently violent event —like a tiger attacking a buffalo—has been frozen in the center of the canvas. Rousseau renders the tropical forest of his imagination in lush, bold colors dominated by several shades of green. He combines plants and animals that are not ordinarily found on the same continent to produce a vivid imaginary world. The most well known of these paintings, a work considered by many to be Rousseau's masterpiece, is *The Dream.* Painted just a few months before he died, this work contains many of the same elements as his other jungle scenes, with one notable difference: in the midst of the tropical forest lies a nude woman on a red sofa. As the title implies, the painting depicts the fantasy landscape the woman was transported to in her dreams. Rousseau named the woman Yadwigha (sometimes the painting is called *Yadwigha's Dream*) after a woman he knew. Apollinaire summed up the response of other painters to this work: "In this painting we find beauty that is indisputable. . . . I don't believe anyone will dare laugh this year. . . . Ask the painters. They are unanimous: they admire."

In the late summer of 1910, when most of Paris was still out of town on summer holiday, Rousseau neglected a cut in his leg until it became infected and gangrenous, or decayed. He went to the hospital and died soon afterward. The hospital mistakenly classified him as an alcoholic, and he was given a poor man's burial. Later, some of his friends contributed to the purchase of a burial plot and a tombstone, on which his epitaph, written by Apollinaire, was carved by eminent Romanian sculptor Constantin Brancusi (1876–1957). Although Rousseau's work had begun to be accepted during his lifetime, the true value of his art was not realized until after his death. The elements of his works that were considered so naive and childlike by contemporary critics are now seen as part of the very foundation of modern art.

For More Information

Books and Periodicals

Grosjean, Didier, and Claudine Roland. *Rousseau: Still Voyages.* New York: Chelsea House Publishers, 1989.

Henri Rousseau. New York: The Museum of Modern Art, 1985.

Schmalenbach, Werner. *Henri Rousseau: Dreams of the Jungle.* Munich: Prestel-Verlag, 1998.

Wernick, Robert. "Rousseau: The Customs Clerk Who Created a World of Wonder." *Smithsonian* 15 (February 1985): p. 80.

Web Sites

"The Imaginary World of Henri Rousseau." *The National Gallery of Art: Washington D.C.* [Online] Available http://www.nga.gov/education/schoolarts/rousseau.htm (last accessed on July 5, 2001).

"Rousseau, Henri." *WebMuseum, Paris.* [Online] Available http://www.ibiblio.org/wm/paint/auth/rousseau/ (last accessed on July 5, 2001).

Betye Saar

Born July 30, 1926
Los Angeles, California

American mixed-media artist

Betye Saar has said that her art is concerned with the past, by which she means both world history and her own personal heritage. A collector of materials such as dolls, clocks, and old photographs, she builds artworks known as assemblages—sculptures made from found objects—suggestive of themes related to her family, to the rituals of other cultures, and to the American civil rights movement. Saar is considered one of the most important African American artists working today. As her career has evolved, her work has increased in size, from objects that can sit on the shelf to "installations," or works that occupy entire galleries.

Saar has three daughters, and two of them, Lezley Saar (1953–) and Alison Saar (1956–), are also prominent artists. While their mother has undoubtedly influenced them, they have distinct styles and attitudes. Lezley paints emotionally and politically disturbing images. Alison draws inspiration from African and folk art and often incorporates human figures in her sculpture. The Saars are one of the most important families in contemporary American art; they have reached this distinction through each Saar following her own creative path. In 1990, a gallery in Los Angeles held a joint exhibition of Betye Saar and Alison Saar's work, and the subtitle of the exhibition, *Secrets, Dialogues, Revelations,* is an apt summary of the Saars' concerns as artists.

A born collector

Betye Irene Saar started collecting things as a young child. She has recalled that on visits to her grandmother in the Watts neighborhood of Los Angeles, California, "I'd go out in the backyard and find bits of glass and stones in the dirt. Sometimes we'd go to the beach and I'd collect little shells and even bits of dirt." These trips to Watts brought her in contact with an early influence on her art—the *Watts Towers* created by Simon Rodia (1879–1965). Rodia, an Italian immigrant, built these soaring structures out of discarded steel junk and found materials such as broken pottery and glass. This strange yet charming work demonstrated to Saar that art could be made out of other people's garbage. Another early artistic influence was **Joseph Cornell** (1903–1972; see entry in volume 3), an American artist who arranged clay pipes, pages torn from books, and other objects in small wooden boxes of his own construction.

Saar attended the University of California at Los Angeles, receiving her degree in 1949. In her quest to find an artistic style for herself, she learned to look beyond the usual sources. Rodia's towers, after all, were folk art made by an untrained artist, and such work was not then exhibited in museums. Despite the emphasis that standard art histories placed on cities such as Florence, Italy; Paris, France; and New York City, other traditions from other cultures have thrived for centuries. African American artists, in particular, have found folk art by "outsider," or untrained, artists from the American South to be more expressive and energetic than the work done in the capitals of European and American art. Folk practices have influenced Saar and her daughters to a great extent, though each has chosen her own favorite styles and characteristics from this vast array of work.

Black Girl's Window (1969). Mixed media assemblage by Betye Saar. 35.75 in x 18 in x 1.5 in. © Betye Saar. Courtesy of Michael Rosenfeld Gallery, New York, NY.

In the 1950s and 1960s, Saar started a family, but the demands of motherhood did not prevent her from continuing her education, and she took graduate courses in history and art at various institutions. The assassination of civil rights leader Martin Luther King, Jr. (1929–1968) and public outcry over racism in American culture had a strong effect on Saar's development as an artist. The works she produced resemble Cornell's boxes, but they also reflect strong political consciousness and identification with the African American community. *Black Girl's Window* (1969) is divided into two halves. The lower half features the silhouette, or shadow, of a girl with her face and hands pressed up against the window, looking out at the world. The upper half of the artwork, which is itself divided into nine squares like a tic-tac-toe board, represents this world. Inside each square is a symbolic or poetic image such as a skeleton or a crescent moon. Saar created *The Liberation of Aunt Jemima* in 1972; Aunt Jemima, the mascot of a brand of breakfast products, was a widely recognized racist stereotype of an obedient black servant, and Saar arranges various representations of this controversial image in her box. Galleries and museums began showing interest in her work and often exhibited it alongside that of other African American artists. In 1977, she provided the illustrations for *Secretary to the Spirits,* a collection of poetry by Ishmael Reed.

Influenced by two kinds of history

Because of Saar's habit of collecting pieces of the past, it was natural that she would develop an interest in the origin and meanings of these objects. This interest took her in two directions: one pointed at her own family history and the other pointed at the history of other cultures. Among other works made up of objects related to her family, Saar's *Record for Hattie* (1975) is dedicated to a great aunt who brought up her mother, and it contains a pincushion, an egg timer, and other objects that belonged to Hattie. Investigations into her ancestry have turned up not only African American ancestors, but also Irish, Native American, Creole, German, and Scottish roots, and she sees her work as belonging to more traditions than just "black art."

Saar has traveled extensively, visiting Africa, Haiti, and Mexico to discover artistic practices that offer an alternative to European painting. She appreciates a quality shared by African, Haitian, and Mexican art—they all have religious or magical uses, instead of merely being objects that the owner enjoys looking at. Noting, for example Haitian fortune-telling, African ancestor worship, and an oddly celebratory attitude toward death in Mexico, Saar has found a way to incorporate a wide variety of styles in the art of assemblage. Assemblages are created when the artist assembles a sculpture out of objects made by somebody else. *Mti* (1973; the title comes from the Swahili word for *wood*) and *House of Ancient Memory* (1989) are assemblages that resemble altarpieces used in foreign religious rituals, though Saar does not herself practice such rituals; she considers herself a Christian.

Saar continues to produce assemblages, but in the 1980s she began experimenting with another, related art form called "installation." Instead of producing pictures that hang on the wall or sculptures that sit on pedestals, installation artists create environments that people experience from every direction. In 1980, she executed *Secrets and Revelations* at the Studio Museum in Harlem, an institution devoted to African American art and culture. Saar brought together a number of her assemblage works and arranged them into an environment, which she further enhanced with candles and incense. The installation *Mojotech* was created during a residence at the Massachusetts Institute of Technology in 1987. Featuring circuit boards and other discarded pieces of old computers, the work seems like a change in direction for the artist, until it becomes clear that in her choice of material she continues to show an interest in memory.

Saar and her daughters

In 1990, Betye Saar collaborated with her daughter Alison on an installation titled *House of Gris Gris.* Inspired by voudun (voodoo) rituals practiced in Haiti, the work consists of a pair of wings, a pile of rocks, and a hut with a tin roof. Visitors to

Secrets, Dialogues, Revelations, a joint exhibition held at the Wight Art Gallery on the campus of the University of California at Los Angeles (UCLA) in 1990, were able to enter the environment mother and daughter created together and to review sketches each had made for the collaboration. The exhibition featured work each artist had done separately, allowing comparisons to be made. At other times, the works of all three Saar women have been seen together.

Alison Saar says she decided to become an artist when her mother introduced her to Rodia's *Watts Towers.* She studied art history at Scripps College in California and completed a thesis on African American folk art. After that, Alison went on to an artistic career independent of Betye's, exhibiting her work in New York galleries since the early 1980s. Alison Saar's sculptures are made of various materials, including wood, tin, and copper, but unlike her mother's works, they tend to resemble human figures. Works such as *Subway Preacher* (1984) and *Snake Charmer* (1985) emerge from personalities and stereotypes (assumptions made about people based on superficial traits) associated with African Americans. Among her most powerful works is the sculpture *Strange Fruit* (1995), which represents a person hanging upside down. The title is taken from a Billie Holiday (1915–1959) song that protested racially motivated lynchings (public executions conducted by angry mobs). Comparing the daughter's work to her mother's, critic Lucy R. Lippard wrote, "Alison Saar's work is more robust and down-to-earth, funkier, dancing in the daylight."

Like her mother and her sister, Lezley Saar has found more inspiration in folk traditions than in the kind of work normally exhibited in art museums. Unlike them, however, she has

Masterworks

1969	*Black Girl's Window* (by Betye Saar)
1972	*The Liberation of Aunt Jemima* (by Betye Saar)
1975	*Record for Hattie* (by Betye Saar)
1984	*Subway Preacher* (by Alison Saar)
1985	*Snake Charmer* (by Alison Saar)
1987	*Mojotech* (by Betye Saar)
1989	*House of Ancient Memory* (by Betye Saar)
1990	*House of Gris Gris* (by Betye Saar and Alison Saar)
1995	*Strange Fruit* (by Alison Saar)
1999	"Tragic Mulatto" series (by Lezley Saar)

concentrated on the medium of painting, creating simple and powerful works, many of them showing human figures. Her "Anomalies" series focuses on people with physical abnormalities, including conjoined twins (also called Siamese twins) and amputees. These works are reminiscent of banners painted for traveling circuses in the early twentieth century. Her perspective is complex, containing both sympathy and horror toward her subjects. Lezley Saar's "Tragic Mulatto" series of paintings focuses on historical figures of mixed racial parentage; more than just a portrait, *Harriet Hemmings, Slave Daughter of Thomas Jefferson* (1999) explores race and asks questions about identity in America.

For More Information

Books

Clothier, Peter. *Betye Saar.* Los Angeles: The Museum of Contemporary Art, 1984.

Shepherd, Elizabeth. *The Art of Betye and Alison Saar: Secrets, Dialogues, Revelations.* Los Angeles: Wight Art Gallery, 1990.

Web Sites

Alison Saar. [Online] Available http://tiger.towson.edu/users/mbonill/Saar.html (last accessed on July 5, 2001).

"Alison Saar." *Phyllis Kind Gallery.* [Online] Available http://www.phylliskind.com/artists/as/index.html (last accessed on July 5, 2001).

"ArtsNet Minnesota: Inner Worlds: Betye Saar." *ArtsConnected.* [Online] Available http://www.artsconnected.org/artsnetmn/inner/saar.html (last accessed on July 5, 2001).

Betye Saar. [Online] Available http://www.bisaar.com/ (last accessed on July 5, 2001).

The Jan Baum Gallery. [Online] Available http://www.jan-baum.com/ (last accessed on July 5, 2001).

"Lezley Saar." *Beitzel Gallery.* [Online] Available http://www.beitzelgallery.com/images/Saar/lsthumbs.htm (last accessed on July 5, 2001).

Eero Saarinen

Born August 20, 1910
Kirkkonummi, Finland

Died September 1, 1961
Ann Arbor, Michigan

American architect and designer

E ero Saarinen followed in the footsteps of his father, Finnish architect Eliel Saarinen (1873–1950), becoming one of the most adventurous architects in America during the period of prosperity that followed World War II (1939–45). Saarinen's optimistic and appealing style celebrated the promise of technology and helped promote the cause of modern architecture in the United States. Born in Finland, he moved to America at age thirteen and strongly identified with the spirit of his adopted country.

Among his most celebrated projects are the General Motors Technical Center in Warren, Michigan; Washington Dulles International Airport in Washington, D.C.; and the Gateway Arch in St. Louis, Missouri. Unlike many architects who design just buildings, Saarinen worked on a small scale, designing furniture, as well as on a larger scale, planning campuses that involved landscape architecture and multiple buildings. He excelled at creating harmony among these elements,

"I was trying to reach for an absolutely permanent form— a high form."

Eero Saarinen, on the Gateway Arch

▲ *Eero Saarinen.*
Reproduced by permission of the Corbis Corporation.

engineering overall spaces that conveyed a sense of order and efficiency. In this enterprise, he was motivated by a belief in the architect's responsibility to promote civilized behavior and attitudes.

A famous father

Eliel Saarinen was one of Finland's most prominent architects, celebrated in his homeland for the design of the Helsinki train station. His reputation spread to America when he came in second place in a highly publicized contest sponsored by the Chicago Tribune Company for the design of its headquarters; many experts thought his proposal superior to that of the first-place winner. He married his business partner's sister, Loja Gesellius, a sculptor, and they encouraged their children in artistic pursuits. Their son, Eero, and daughter, Pipsan, showed talent from a young age. At twelve, Eero Saarinen (pronounced SAR-un-nun) won a national award for creating a structure of matchsticks. The following year, the family moved to America and soon settled in the suburbs of Detroit, Michigan, so that Eliel could design the buildings on the campus of the Cranbook Foundation, a private school located in Bloomfield Hills. The Saarinens remained in America, and Eliel later served as Cranbrook's president and then as head of its architecture department.

The whole family participated in Cranbrook's design, with Eero Saarinen handling the furniture while his mother worked on the rugs and his sister decorated the auditorium and dining hall. Altogether, it provided the ideal setting for Eero Saarinen's early training in the arts. The institution brought together artists from many disciplines for workshops and intense discussions about the purpose of art. Initially, he wanted to become a sculptor, but by the time he enrolled in Yale University, he had decided to follow his father into the field of architecture. Upon graduation in 1934, he spent two years traveling throughout Europe, touring cities and experiencing architectural masterpieces firsthand. He returned to Michigan as an instructor at Cranbrook and as a partner in his father's architectural firm.

Searches for a style

The father-and-son partnership of Saarinen and Saarinen took on a series of high-profile church and school projects. In 1939, they entered and won a competition to design the art gallery of the Smithsonian Institution in Washington, D.C., but to their disappointment the building was never constructed. During this time, Eero Saarinen married Lily Swann, a Cranbook ceramics student, and befriended Charles Eames (1907–1978), a promising young designer from St. Louis, Missouri, who idolized Eliel Saarinen. The elder Saarinen's style was considered modern and progressive by American standards. Both younger designers, however, were conscious of a wave of designers who had fled Nazi Germany for America. Walter Gropius (1883–1969; see entry in volume 1) and Ludwig Mies van der Rohe (1886–1969), two figures associated with a new school of architecture and design, advocated forms that echoed machines rather than nature. Efficiency was celebrated and decoration was virtually eliminated in what became known as the "international style." In 1940, Eames and Eero Saarinen jointly designed a chair out of plywood (made of sheets of wood glued together, thus creating a material stronger and more flexible than regular wood) that reflected their interest in the international style.

During World War II, Saarinen moved to Washington, D.C., to serve the United States in the Organization for Strategic Services, a branch that later became the Central Intelligence Agency (CIA). Returning to Michigan after the war, he rejoined his father's practice and began preliminary work on a series of projects for General Motors, one of the nation's largest car manufacturers. Due to uncertain economic conditions, these plans were temporarily suspended, and Saarinen and Saarinen turned to designing college campuses in Illinois, Iowa, and Missouri. The U.S. government had recently decided to pay the tuition of soldiers returning from the war, so campuses had to grow to accommodate the influx. Saarinen regarded college campuses as "the oases of our desert-like civilization"—vibrant communities where architecture could foster education and cooperation. Such projects allowed him to engage in community planning, an activity concerned with not just a single building but with the everyday living and working situations of a group of people. In a university community, for instance, students, faculty, and administrators interact in classrooms, in offices, and on park benches, all designed by a community planner.

Designs the arch for St. Louis

Saarinen had great respect for his father, but as time went on, he found himself disagreeing with aspects of his architectural philosophy. Eliel clung to traditional architecture while Eero embraced the international style and up-to-date materials and techniques. In 1947, when the city of St. Louis held a competition to find a designer for a project known as the Jefferson Westward Expansion Memorial, father and son decided to submit separate entries. The project was meant to honor Thomas Jefferson (1743–1826), third president of the United States and an architect by training. One of Jefferson's accomplishments as president was the Louisiana Purchase (1803), which greatly expanded the country to the west. In considering how to capture the spirit of this historic moment, Saarinen rejected his father's preference for a conventional monument in favor of a soaring arch that would serve as "gateway to the West." (The Gateway Arch later became its unofficial name.) Rather than stone or marble, the monument would be made of stainless steel, a recently invented building material. As it happened, a telegram was sent congratulating Eliel Saarinen, but a few days later a correction was issued: the winner of the contest was not the father but the son. Standing 630 feet wide at its base and 630 feet tall, Eero Saarinen's monument has become a landmark and a symbol of progress, visited by more than four million people annually. The innovative elevator inside the arch was designed by an engineer named Dick Bowser.

Meanwhile, America was experiencing an era of prosperity, and economic prospects improved for General Motors. The company revived its plan for a large and modern technical center and approved Saarinen's vision for the building complex

The Gateway Arch, St. Louis, Missouri. Designed by Eero Saarinen. Photograph reproduced by permission of James Blank.

and its surrounding landscape. Eliel Saarinen died in 1950, and his son assumed command of the project, taking as his inspiration the campus of the Illinois Institute of Technology (IIT) designed by Mies van der Rohe. While some critics argue that the overall design of the project does not hold together as well as IIT, it includes some superbly designed features, including a spiral staircase in the Research Administration Building and a rectangular reflecting pool. As Saarinen's reputation grew, he was given more opportunities to work on projects that fell under the category of community planning. In 1953, the architect and his wife divorced; Saarinen then married art critic Aline B. Louchheim. He had two children with his first wife and one with his second.

Le Corbusier

Le Corbusier (1887–1965; kor-buze-YAY) is one of the biggest names in modern architecture, revered as one of the figures who liberated buildings from the bonds of the past. Declaring "a house is a machine for living in," he strove to eliminate ornamentation in favor of what he termed a purely functional approach to architecture. Nevertheless, the buildings he designed look less like machines than rough-hewn modern sculptures.

Born as Charles-Édouard Jeanneret in Switzerland in 1887, he left school at age thirteen to study at the École des Arts Décoratifs (School of Decorative Arts). An influential teacher introduced him to art history and later advised him to become an architect. For awhile, Jeanneret worked as a painter and with designer Amédée Ozenfant (1886–1966) formed a magazine devoted to modern art. In the 1920s, he adopted a new name suggested by his collaborator, based on a relative's name, and thereafter Le Corbusier concentrated on architecture.

During his long career, Le Corbusier published numerous books on the subject of modern architecture and designed challenging and futuristic buildings. The Citrohan House of 1922 is supported by pillars, so that the ground underneath is free. This project also features a roof terrace and a plain

Le Corbusier. Courtesy of the Library of Congress.

facade, design hallmarks of his later work. A later masterpiece, the chapel Notre-Dame-du-Haut at Ronchamp (1950–55) departs from the strict rules he had set forth for architecture, notably in its massive and sculptural roof. Both projects, however, seem to revel in the freedoms afforded by concrete, a strong and versatile material that continued to be associated with Le Corbusier after his death in 1965.

Looks at the big picture—and the details, too

Most of the projects over the remainder of Saarinen's career involved multiple buildings and considerations of such issues as lawns and traffic, both automotive and pedestrian. The plaza he built for Massachusetts Institute of Technology in 1955 contained an auditorium and chapel carefully laid out among trees planted in even rows. The following year, he designed two separate complexes of buildings for IBM, then known by its full name, International Business Machines—one in Rochester, Minnesota, and one in Yorktown, New York. A commission from Bell Telephone Laboratories in Holmdel, New Jersey, came soon after that. He approached all three projects with the conviction that his architectural ideals were perfectly suited for science and technology, pursuits that defined American life in the 1950s. Saarinen's plans for these facilities, as usual, took into account various considerations ranging from how they appeared when approached by car to how easily workers from different departments could communicate with each other to where they should sit. He designed what became known as pedestal furniture, including the so-called Tulip Chair, both to echo the forms of his buildings and to contribute to the sense of bold technological progress.

After working on the TWA terminal at New York's La Guardia Airport, Saarinen began working on the Dulles International Airport in Washington, D.C., one of the final projects of his career. Named for American diplomat John Foster Dulles (pronounced DULL-iss; 1888–1959), this work has been called his masterpiece. A dramatically sloping roof distinguishes this massive structure, which nevertheless projects a sense of lightness. The roof, made of concrete slabs resting on steel cables, is a marvel of engineering. He encountered a num-

Masterworks	
1947	Womb Chair
1947–48	Jefferson Westward Expansion Memorial (The Gateway Arch)
1951–57	General Motors Technical Center
1956	Tulip Chair
1956–62	TWA Terminal, New York
1961–62	Dulles International Airport

ber of design challenges in the planning phase, among them, the great distances between runways required for jet airplanes, a new invention at the time. Saarinen's solution was a "mobile lounge," a waiting area on wheels that saved passengers from having to walk long distances.

Eero Saarinen died of a brain tumor in 1961, leaving many projects uncompleted. Construction on his famous arch was not finished until February 28, 1965. His influence can be seen in many buildings today, as well as in the relatively young field of urban planning. Urban planners, people who try to solve transportation and other problems associated with cities, follow Saarinen's lead by thinking on a large scale and by attempting to improve people's lives through efficient design.

For More Information

Books

Cheek, Larry. *Eero Saarinen: Architect, Sculptor, Visionary.* St. Louis: Jefferson National Expansion Historical Association, 1998.

Saarinen, Eliel. *The Search for Form in Art and Architecture.* Mineola, NY: Dover, 1985.

Temko, Allan. *Eero Saarinen.* New York: George Braziller, 1962.

Web Sites

"Eero Saarinen." *Great Buildings Online.* [Online] Available http://www.greatbuildings.com/gbc/architects/Eero_Saarinen.html (last accessed on July 5, 2001).

"Eero Saarinen." *Scandinavian Design.* [Online] Available http://www.scandinaviandesign.com/eero_saarinen/ (last accessed on July 5, 2001).

"Jefferson National Expansion Memorial." *National Park Service.* [Online] Available http://www.nps.gov/jeff/ (last accessed on July 5, 2001).

John Singer Sargent

Born January 12, 1856
Florence, Italy

Died April 15, 1925
Boston, Massachusetts

American painter

John Singer Sargent is famous for his elegant portraits of the men and women of high society, even though his artistic ambitions lay elsewhere. He preferred painting nature and appreciated the innovations of the French impressionists. No matter how hard he tried to escape portraiture, however, the genre continued to catch up to him. Sargent's *Madame X* and his portrait of his friend, writer Henry James (1843–1916), capture the spirit of the wealthiest segment of society in London, England; Paris, France; and New England in the late nineteenth and early twentieth centuries.

Although Sargent's society patrons welcomed him, he never felt completely at ease in their company. He kept his distance in all social situations and never felt truly at home in either America or Europe. Sargent's emotionally detached perspective helped him to identify the true personalities of the sitters. The patrons usually found the portraits flattering, a fact that made Sargent rich but, perhaps, unhappy.

"Ask me to paint your shutters, your doors, or your walls . . . but do not ask me to paint the human form."

Letter to a potential portrait client, 1907

▲ **Self Portrait *(1892).* Painting by John Singer Sargent.** *Photograph by Francis G. Mayer. Reproduced by permission of the Corbis Corporation.*

Expatriate beginnings

To lead an "expatriate" existence means to live away from your homeland, and the word describes John Singer Sargent's life right from the start. His parents left Philadelphia, Pennsylvania, and relocated to Florence, Italy, just a few months before he was born. FitzWilliam Sargent was a doctor, and his wife, Mary, grew bored easily and suffered from numerous minor ailments. Remaining in Europe was her idea. John was the second of six children, but his elder sister did not survive infancy. The Sargent family was not wealthy, which might explain why the artist was never comfortable around wealth.

Restless like his mother, John could not sit still to do schoolwork, but he enjoyed learning about plants and animals. When the family temporarily relocated to Dresden, Germany, in 1871, he was sixteen years old, and he began to take drawing seriously, spending hours sketching plaster casts of classical sculpture. Travels to Venice revealed to him the achievements of sixteenth-century masters Titian (c. 1488–1576; see entry in volume 2) and Tintoretto (c. 1518–1594). The Sargents moved to Paris in 1874.

An influential teacher

In Paris, Sargent joined the studio of Carolus-Duran (c. 1837–1917; born as Charles-Emile-Auguste Durand), a successful young painter with a flamboyant personality. Carolus-Duran won attention for dressing his portrait subjects in elaborate costumes. He was friends with Claude Monet (1840–1926; see entry in volume 2) and Edouard Manet (1832–1883; see entry in volume 2) and, although Sargent's reputation is now somewhat overshadowed by these peers, his fame exceeded theirs in their lifetimes. Sargent, one of about twenty students in the studio of Carolus-Duran, quickly became the teacher's favorite. He won a number of local prizes, accomplishments for which his teacher claimed credit.

Although he always considered himself American, Sargent did not travel to the United States until 1876. The experience of visiting Philadelphia relatives was uncomfortable, and this so-called homecoming made him feel more foreign than ever. He returned to Paris and to the studio of Carolus-Duran, but by this time he was attempting paintings that were more ambitious than anything that had been attempted by his teacher—simplifying and streamlining the figures for a more "modern" effect.

Launches his career

At the start of 1877, when Sargent was twenty-one years old, he completed the portrait of Fanny Watts, another American living in Europe. The picture was well-regarded, and Sargent's term with his teacher came to an end. With his Paris connections and his talents, he could have continued making portraits and earning a steady income, but he wanted to try other kinds of painting and to see more of the world.

The three versions he completed of *Fishing for Oysters at Cancale,* a scene of peasants on the beach rather than an aristocrat in a drawing room, were a departure, but not a radical one. To challenge himself it was necessary to leave France, and he set out for Spain. The spectacle of Spanish dancers inspired him, and the sketches he made in 1879 eventually led to the 1882 painting *El Jaleo,* a Spanish word that means "loud noise." The dancer in the foreground is caught in an exotic pose, while a row of musicians behind her strum furiously. His travels also took him to the North African countries of Morocco and Tunisia.

Sargent admired the dark tones and lively composition of Spanish painter Diego Velázquez (1599–1660; see entry in volume 2), and his influence shows not just in the Spanish-themed works but in the paintings he completed upon his return to France; *The Boit Children,* a group portrait of the four daughters of Boston lawyer Edward Darley Boit, intentionally resembles Velázquez's 1656 masterpiece *Last Meninas.* Writing in *Harper's* magazine, novelist Henry James called *The Boit Children* "astonishing."

Although Sargent tried to balance portraiture with other kinds of work, his portraits consistently won him acclaim. For Americans in Paris looking to have their picture done, he was their first choice. *Dr. Samuel Jean Pozzi at Home* (1881) is a full-length study of a prominent gynecologist in a bright red

Madame X (1884).
Painting by John Singer
Sargent. Oil on canvas.
82⅛ x 43¼ in.
Metropolitan Museum of
Art, New York.
Photograph reproduced
by permission of the
Corbis Corporation.

robe. *Lady with the Rose* (1882), another full-length portrait, shows Charlotte Louise Burkhardt, a young woman who almost won Sargent's heart. His biographers report that he lost his nerve and did not pursue the romance. The subject has a simultaneously dignified and familiar bearing; she seems to be staring at the painter impatiently.

Paints the controversial *Madame X*

Although she is now known as "Madame X," the identity of the woman who posed for Sargent's most notorious portrait was never a secret. She was born Virginie Avegno in Louisiana. After her father died in the Civil War (1861–65), she and her family moved to Paris, and when she grew up she married banker Pierre Gautreau. She was beautiful, and she knew that her extraordinarily pale complexion attracted attention. Whether from jealousy or some other cause, French society did not look kindly upon Madame Gautreau.

Captivated by her beauty, Sargent enthusiastically began painting her portrait in 1883. He had her pose in many different positions before he settled on one: standing, with her face turned sharply to the left to reveal her dramatic profile. When the painting came on view at the Salon (government-sponsored exhibition) of 1884, there was a terrific outcry at what the public construed as the bold sexuality displayed by Madame Gautreau—her shoulders were exposed and her dress was cut very low. While most of the criticism was directed at the subject and not the artist, Sargent, who was used to steady praise, took it personally. As the years went by, however, he came to take great pride in this portrait.

Ventures to London

Restless as always, Sargent traveled to London in 1884, where his reputation preceded him and where a different type of clientele awaited him. Instead of people who were born into money, these were "industrialists," people who had made money in railroads and other industries that arose in the nineteenth century. For such clients, many of whom came from humble backgrounds, portraits were a way of attaining class and credibility. Henry James befriended Sargent and introduced him to industrialists (this class of people frequently appeared in his novels), who appreciated Sargent's genteel and businesslike manners.

Sargent also found time to paint novelist Robert Louis Stevenson (1850–1894), who was then about to publish his famous tale of a split personality, *The Strange Case of Dr. Jekyll and Mr. Hyde.* In the picture, the writer paces the floor, twirling his mustache, while his wife Fanny slouches in a chair nearby, a colorful scarf draped over her head.

In London, Sargent was taken with the work of the pre-Raphaelites, a "brotherhood of artists whose work had an ornate, flowery quality despite their claims of reviving the simple style of religious art that came before Italian Renaissance master **Raphael** (1483–1520; see entry in volume 4). Sargent's *Carnation, Lily, Lily, Rose* (1885), a painting that is both literally and figuratively "flowery," shows the pre-Raphaelite influence. This popular picture of two little girls lighting paper lanterns was completed shortly after Sargent suffered a minor head wound in a diving incident.

Other ambitions

Sargent continued making portraits into the first decade of the twentieth century, notably the stunning *Lady Agnew of Lochnaw* (1892–93), and his fortunes and praise continued to pile up. Sculptor Auguste Rodin (1840–1917; see entry in volume 2) called him "the Vandyke of our age," referring to seventeenth-century Flemish court painter Sir Anthony Vandyke (1599–1641). However, Sargent kept trying other genres, especially nature painting, and grew increasingly interested in the technical advances put forth by the impressionists. The picture *Claude Monet Painting* (1887) captures one of the leading figures of this movement and displays a familiarity with Monet's style, that is, energetic brushstrokes and a sensitivity to the effects of sunlight. Monet acknowledged Sargent's skill but never admitted him into the impressionists' inner circle, possibly because the American had not "paid his dues" with the rest of the group—enduring harsh reviews, public dismay, and so on.

In 1890, Sargent sailed to America and was commissioned to paint murals on the walls of the Boston Public Library, which was being built by the prestigious architectural firm McKim, Mead & White. The opportunity to tackle a serious subject stimulated him, and he planned an elaborate series on the theme of the history of religion. Collaborating with the architects, Sargent embellished the work with metal, paper, jewels, stenciled borders, and relief sculptures (this kind of sculpture is carved out of a flat surface). Although his efforts achieved instant success, in the long run the murals have not added to Sargent's reputation.

In 1907, Sargent promised to himself not to do any more portraits. "What a nuisance," he complained to a friend, "having to entertain the sitter and to look happy when one feels wretched." He generally kept this promise, creating nature scenes and paintings based on literary or historic themes, but occasionally he gave in to demands of portrait clients who were either friends or very important people. The latter category included wealthy industrialist John D. Rockefeller (1839–1937) and U.S. presidents Theodore Roosevelt (1858–1919) and Woodrow Wilson (1856–1924). In 1913, Sargent was commissioned by some friends of Henry James to execute the novelist's portrait as a seventieth birthday present. The author loved the resulting painting; his head seems to glow against a gloomy background. Unfortunately, when the picture was first exhibited in May of 1914, a deranged person slashed the canvas with a knife. It was soon restored and now hangs in London's National Portrait Gallery.

Sargent's last important picture is not a portrait but a war painting. *Gassed* (1919) was executed for the Hall of Remembrance, a war memorial in London. Sargent had witnessed a group of World War I (1914–18) soldiers engulfed in a cloud of mustard gas, and this became the subject of the uncharacteristically brutal painting. The artist died in London in 1925, a few days before he was scheduled to sail for Boston to work on another mural commission.

For More Information

Books

Olson, Stanley. *John Singer Sargent: His Portrait.* New York: St. Martin's Press, 1986.

Ormond, Richard, and Elaine Kilmurray, eds. *John Singer Sargent.* Princeton, NJ: Princeton University Press, 1998.

Ratcliff, Carter. *Sargent.* New York: Abbeville, 1986.

Web Sites

"John Singer Sargent." *Artcyclopedia* [Online] Available http://www.artcyclopedia.com/artists/sargent_john_singer.html (last accessed on July 5, 2001).

The John Singer Sargent Virtual Gallery. [Online] Available http://home.talkcity.com/EaselSt/johnsingersargent/ (last accessed on July 5, 2001).

"Sargent Murals at the Boston Public Library." *Harvard University Art Museums.* [Online] Available http://www.artmuseums.harvard.edu/sargentatharvard/bplmural/bpl.html (last accessed on July 5, 2001).

Egon Schiele

Born June 12, 1890
Tulln, Austria
Died October 31, 1918
Vienna, Austria

**Austrian painter,
draftsman, printmaker**

His life cut short before he turned thirty years old, Egon Schiele had an artistic career that lasted just over a decade. The works he left behind, however—thousands of drawings and hundreds of paintings—indicate that he approached his art with a singular energy and purpose. His works reveal a staggering emotional intensity and a willingness to expose all facets of human nature, from noble to sleazy. His artistic explorations of human sexuality caused a sensation during his lifetime (he was even briefly imprisoned on an obscenity charge) and still have the power to shock. Unsatisfied with the traditional approach of Vienna's academic art community, Schiele took his work in a new direction, in the process becoming a leader of the movement known as Austrian expressionism. Expressionists rejected the conventional belief that art should portray the world in a realistic fashion; instead, they felt art's purpose was to express the artist's emotions above all else. Using dramatic, angular lines and dark colors, Schiele and other expressionists used their art to com-

"How great must be your joy . . . to have given birth to me."

Egon Schiele, in a letter to his mother, March 1913

▲ Self-Portrait in Shirt (1910). Painting by Egon Schiele.
© Austrian Archives. Reproduced by permission of the Corbis Corporation.

municate the fear, beauty, anxiety, and ugliness that they perceived in the modern world.

A troubled childhood

Egon Leo Adolf Schiele (pronounced SHEE-luh) was the only son born to Adolf and Marie Schiele. His mother had been pregnant three times with boys prior to Egon's birth, but each of those babies was stillborn (dead at birth). He had three sisters, though the eldest died when she was ten years old. Perhaps the most significant detail of Schiele's childhood was that his father had syphilis, a sexually transmitted infection that, if left untreated, can lead to insanity and death. Adolf passed the disease on to his wife, who suffered its effects firsthand as well as having to deal with her husband's mental and physical deterioration. From the windows of his home, the young Schiele could see the railroad station where his father worked. Perhaps as an escape from an unhappy family life, he spent his time drawing trains, exhibiting a remarkable talent. In 1904, when Schiele was fourteen years old, his father died. In spite of the fact that his father had become increasingly violent and unpredictable as the disease progressed, Schiele was devastated by his death and remembered him as a good man.

At age sixteen, Schiele easily passed the entrance exam for the Vienna Academy of Fine Arts, and he persuaded his mother and uncle (who had become his legal guardian after his father's death) to allow him to enroll there. He received a traditional education, honing his drawing skills and learning all about the classical art of ancient Greece and Rome. But the restless and imaginative Schiele soon grew frustrated with the school's conservative attitude and opposition to modern art. In his second year at the Academy, he prepared some drawings on his own and brought them to the studio of celebrated Viennese artist **Gustav Klimt** (1862–1918; see entry in volume 3). Klimt pronounced that the younger man did indeed have talent, and thus began a lifelong friendship. The younger artist looked up to Klimt, whose earlier rebellious break with Vienna's art establishment inspired Schiele to engage in a rebellion of his own.

In 1909, he left the Academy to join with other progressive young artists in the *Neukunstgruppe,* or New Art Group. He produced such noteworthy works as a portrait of his beloved sister, who had modeled for him since childhood. The style of *Gerti Schiele* reveals the artist's admiration for the works of Klimt, among others, but it also indicates a unique emerging talent. Klimt offered more than just praise for Schiele: he helped him get work with the important design group called Wiener Werkstätte, and he encouraged him to exhibit several works at the 1909 Vienna International Exhibition. With Klimt as his mentor and feeling a newfound sense of self-confidence, even arrogance, Schiele began his career as an artist.

A controversial adulthood

While some of his early works show an obvious debt to Klimt's decorative style, Schiele also found inspiration in the works of other artists, including Dutch painter Vincent van Gogh (1853–1890; see entry in volume 1) and Norway's **Edvard Munch** (1863–1944; see entry in volume 4). He painted numerous landscapes and cityscapes, but Schiele's primary interest was painting the human body. He was particularly intrigued by self-portraits, in which he consistently portrayed himself in a somewhat negative light. His self-portraits, such as *Self-Portrait Clothed* (1910), highlight his fears and weaknesses—showing him with red-rimmed eyes, a scrawny body, yellow skin, and sometimes, chopped off limbs—while at the same time revealing his endless fascination with looking at himself. Schiele applied the same critical eye to his other models. Rather than following the traditional notion of an artist showing his subjects at their best, Schiele revealed the whole person: both the beautiful and the repulsive, the elegant and the vulgar, the graceful and the awkward. He used jagged, angular lines and somber colors to reveal psychological as well as physical characteristics of his models. Unlike many artists of his time, Schiele openly explored his models' sexuality, painting them in provocative poses, frequently nude or half-nude.

A Questionable History: Artworks Stolen in Nazi Germany

As the Nazi Party seized power in the years before World War II (1939–45), the Jewish citizens of Germany and other nations under Nazi control were stripped of their basic human rights and their possessions before being deported to concentration camps where six million Jews were killed. Among the items most vigorously pursued by Adolf Hitler (1889–1945) and the Nazis were thousands of valuable paintings, drawings, and other artworks owned by German Jewish families.

In the years following the war, these artworks made their way to countries throughout Europe and North America. Many are still missing, but some have turned up in the world's most prestigious museums, auction houses, and private collections. The people and institutions that acquire such works do not generally realize that they were stolen from victims of the Holocaust. Critics suggest, however, that careful research into a work's provenance, or history of ownership, would reveal clues indicating there may have been questionable activity concerning that work before, during, and just after the war.

Many Holocaust survivors and their families have searched for decades for works stolen from them by the Nazi government. While discovering the whereabouts of such artworks can be difficult and time-consuming, actually getting the works back has proven even more difficult. Two disputed paintings by Egon Schiele, *Portrait of Wally* (1912) and *Dead City III* (1911), were at the center of legal battles in 1998. The ownership claims of two families—who said the works had been unlawfully taken from their relatives by the Nazis—conflicted with those of the Austrian government, which declared that the works had been legally obtained. In another case, an American woman—the last surviving heir of an Austrian art dealer and Holocaust victim named Ferdinand Bloch-Bauer—sued the Austrian government and the National Gallery of Austria for the return of six paintings by Gustav Klimt that she claims were stolen from Bloch-Bauer. Such complicated cases are not likely to be resolved quickly or easily.

While Schiele's works did stir up some controversy, they also earned considerable praise. Within a few years of leaving the Academy, his reputation had spread throughout Vienna and to other major European cities, and he came to be seen as a representative of the younger generation of Austrian expression-

ists. Even as his works gained acceptance, his unconventional personal life proved scandalous. In 1911, Schiele began living with a seventeen-year-old woman, Valerie Neuzil (known as Walli; also spelled Wally), who had modeled for him many times. Desperately poor and eager to escape big-city life, Schiele and Walli moved to a small town outside Vienna called Neulengbach. The town's conservative residents did not approve of Schiele and Walli living together while unmarried, nor did they appreciate the sexual nature of the artist's works. In April 1912, Schiele was arrested for what was considered an immoral and obscene lifestyle. He spent more than three weeks in jail, during which time he obtained painting supplies and created some of his most powerful works. Filled with bitterness, anxiety, and self-pity, Schiele translated his feelings into such tortured works as *For My Art and for My Loved Ones I Will Gladly Endure to the End.*

Although best known for his drawings of people, Schiele also produced highly regarded landscapes and cityscapes. These works display Schiele's characteristic angular lines and bold colors, but the despair and anger that make his portraits so recognizable are minimized. Most of his town paintings are empty of people, and though he described them as "dead towns," the mood of such paintings as *Stein on the Danube* and *Krumau on the Moldau ("The Small City")* (both 1913) is far less somber than his portraits. In *Edge of Town* (1917), one of the few cityscapes that also includes human figures, the atmosphere is almost joyful. Covered in geometric patches of bright colors, these works seem to have been produced by an artist more at peace than the Schiele who painted, for example, *Death and Maiden (Self Portrait with Walli).*

A premature demise

Schiele's imprisonment in Neulengbach left him feeling angry and abused, convinced that he was misunderstood and had been unjustly punished. He became increasingly isolated from society and poured his anguish into his works. His personal struggles did not slow down the progress of his career (and in fact they may have fueled it, as the passions he felt resulted in powerful, dramatic art). He held exhibitions throughout Austria and in Italy and France, even receiving a career retrospective at a gallery in Munich, Germany, a rare honor for an artist so young. In 1914, Schiele met Edith Harms, a young, middle-class woman who lived with her family across the street from the artist's studio. Schiele pursued and eventually proposed marriage to

Edith. She accepted, and they were married in June 1915. A few days later, in the midst of World War I (1914–18), Schiele was drafted into the military. Due to his status as a celebrated artist, Schiele was able to avoid combat duty, and his new wife could occasionally join him at his postings.

In spite of the war, Schiele's career flourished. He had successful shows in museums and galleries, and he finally began to achieve some financial success. The security provided by his growing income and by his marriage lent his works a new measure of calm and even tenderness. Schiele's wife became pregnant, and the artist affectionately sketched her portrait. Their contentment did not last long, however, as Edith, six months pregnant, came down with influenza in late October 1918. The deadly strain of the virus had reached pandemic proportions, meaning that huge outbreaks occurred all over the world. The influenza pandemic killed more than twenty million people before running its course in the spring of 1919. Edith succumbed to the illness on October 28, and three days later, Schiele, too, was dead. Schiele's death at age twenty-eight has left scholars to forever speculate how his style would have developed over time. In the years since his death, the emotional intensity he brought to his works has not dimmed. His portrayals of human anguish and desire have proven meaningful and compelling for every generation that has followed.

For More Information

Books

Comini, Alessandra. *Egon Schiele's Portraits.* Berkeley: University of California Press, 1990.

Whitford, Frank. *Egon Schiele* (World of Art series). London: Thames & Hudson, 1985.

Web Sites

"Art Channel Exhibition: Egon Schiele." *Art Channel.* [Online] Available http://www.art4.net/EXPOes.htm (last accessed on July 5, 2001).

"The Artist and His Work." *The Museum of Modern Art.* [Online] Available http://www.moma.org/exhibitions/schiele/artistwork.html (last accessed on July 5, 2001).

"Egon Schiele." *Mark Harden's Artchive.* [Online] Available http://artchive.com/artchive/S/schiele.html (last accessed on July 5, 2001).

"Schiele, Egon." *WebMuseum, Paris.* [Online] Available http://www.ibiblio.org/wm/paint/auth/schiele/ (last accessed on June 8, 2001).

Maurice Sendak

Born June 10, 1928
Brooklyn, New York

American illustrator, writer, artist,
set and costume designer

A s the author or illustrator of more than eighty books for children, notably *Where the Wild Things Are* and *In the Night Kitchen,* Maurice Sendak has touched the lives of millions. His works, while beloved by generations of children, have been criticized for portraying frightening situations too candidly and for exploring the darker emotions and impulses children have. Supporters, however, praise Sendak for honestly and respectfully addressing children's emotional lives. The children in his books are realistic, flesh-and-blood creations—kids who misbehave and feel anger and frustration toward their parents and siblings—rather than purely sweet and innocent beings. In addition to his award-winning books, Sendak has also distinguished himself as a costume and set designer for major opera productions.

Brooklyn as seen from a window

Born and raised in Brooklyn, New York, Maurice Bernard Sendak was the youngest of three children born to Philip and

"All of us collect fortunes when we are children—a fortune of colors, of lights and darkness, of movements, of tensions."

▲ *Maurice Sendak.*
Reproduced by permission of Archive Photos.

Sarah Sendak. He was a frail child, prone to sickness, and he later remembered his youth as "one long series of illnesses." His loving but overprotective parents, Jewish immigrants from Poland, tried to shelter their youngest child from further illness by keeping him indoors much of the time. Sendak watched the neighborhood kids playing from his apartment windows, compensating for his loneliness by reading comic books (Mickey Mouse was his favorite) and making drawings of the other kids' activities. His love of storytelling originates with his father, who entertained his children with colorful and often hair-raising stories based on myths, fairy tales, and the Old Testament. When he was nine years old, Sendak received his first real book, a gift from his sister. His love for the book— *The Prince and the Pauper,* by Mark Twain (1835–1910)— went beyond the story written on its pages. He loved the look, feel, and even smell of the book. Books were very special to the young Sendak, and that passionate feeling continued into his adult life, when he oversaw every detail of his books' design, from front cover to back.

As children, Sendak and his brother Jack wrote and illustrated many tales based on family members and people from the neighborhood. (Jack also became an author of children's books as an adult, and Sendak has illustrated two of them.) While in high school, Sendak created his own comic strip for the school newspaper and illustrated a physics textbook for one of his teachers. Against his father's wishes, Sendak did not go to college after graduating from high school. Instead, he worked at the Manhattan warehouse of a window display company, helping to construct the models for store displays. He met a number of other young artists at that time, people who worked at the warehouse to make a living while developing their craft at night. In the summer of 1948, Sendak quit that job, and, back at home with his parents in Brooklyn, spent his time making sketches of neighborhood kids. That summer, he and his brother Jack began designing and crafting wooden mechanical toys based on scenes from nursery rhymes and fairy tales. In the hopes of selling a whole line of toys, they presented their models to F. A. O. Schwarz, a huge toy store on Fifth Avenue in Manhattan. While their toys were considered too expensive to produce and sell for profit, Sendak's artistic abilities impressed the window-display director, who offered him a job.

While working at F. A. O. Schwarz, Sendak attended evening classes at the Art Students League. Although he had always been uncomfortable in the structured environment of school, he enjoyed his art classes at the League and confirmed his desire to become a professional illustrator of children's books. He acquainted himself with the works of some of the best illustrators in the world by browsing through F. A. O. Schwarz's book department. Learning of his talents and hopes, the buyer for the book department arranged for Sendak to meet an important children's-book editor, Ursula Nordstrom, one day in 1950. Looking at some of his drawings, Nordstrom immediately recognized Sendak's gift, and she called him the next day to ask him to illustrate a children's book called *The Wonderful Farm.* This event marked the beginning of one of the happiest and most productive periods in Sendak's career. Nordstrom nurtured his talent, taught him about the publishing industry, and encouraged him to master a variety of styles so he could illustrate many different kinds of books. Soon after he began working with Nordstrom, Sendak was asked to illustrate a book called *A Hole Is to Dig* (1952) by Ruth Krauss. This almost-missed opportunity (a well-known illustrator had been asked first but turned down the project) became Sendak's first major success and the springboard for many subsequent achievements.

A full-fledged illustrator

The success of *A Hole Is to Dig,* with critics singling out his illustrations for praise, gave Sendak the push he needed to move into his own apartment and quit his job at the toy store. While he was too busy illustrating in those early years to work on any writing projects, Sendak continued to collect ideas for his own works while drawing pictures for those of others. After a few years, and with the encouragement of Nordstrom, Sendak began work on a story that he would write and illustrate. *Kenny's Window* (1956), while not entirely satisfying to Sendak, contains many of the themes and ideas that populate his best works. As Sendak described it in Selma Lanes's book

Dr. Seuss

One of the most beloved children's book authors and illustrators of all time, Dr. Seuss created the catchy rhymes, silly nonsense words, and imaginary characters of such classics as *Cat in the Hat, Green Eggs and Ham,* and *The Lorax.* Theodor Seuss Geisel (1904–1991) invented fantastic creatures—occasionally resembling real animals but primarily coming from his vivid imagination—whose silly antics amused kids as well as subtly taught them about colors, counting, helping others, and respecting the environment.

Geisel did not grow up thinking he would become an artist. In his first art class, in fact, his teacher informed him that he would never learn to draw. He continued to practice without formal instruction, though, and in the process developed his unique style. Geisel started his career writing and illustrating for magazines such as *Life* and *Vanity Fair.* He published his first children's book—*And to Think That I Saw It on Mulberry Street*—in 1937. During World War II (1939–45), Geisel and his wife Helen created two short films, *Hitler Lives* and *Design for Death,* to support the cause of the Allied countries (which included the United States, England, France, and the Soviet Union). These films later won Academy Awards for best documentary subjects.

In addition to earning nearly every major award given to writers of chil-

Dr. Seuss (Theodor Geisel). © James L. Amos. Reproduced by permission of the Corbis Corporation.

dren's books, Geisel won the hearts of millions of young readers. The simple yet lively text and quirky drawings of books like *Cat in the Hat* (1957) and *Hop on Pop* (1963) pull even reluctant readers into the tales. Geisel felt strongly that a story for kids should contain a moral. Referring to *How the Grinch Stole Christmas,* he explained that "if the Grinch steals Christmas, . . . he has to bring it back in the end." He did admit, however, that while writing that story, "I was kind of rooting for the Grinch."

The Art of Maurice Sendak, Kenny and many of his other characters "are held back by life, but, one way or another, manage miraculously to find release from their troubles." The simple pen-and-ink drawings of this book play a secondary role to the thought-provoking story, and looking back on them years later Sendak described the drawings as "ghastly."

A few years later, Sendak published *The Sign on Rosie's Door,* a book based on a real girl that he had spent many hours as a young man watching and sketching from the window of his family's Brooklyn apartment. Rosie—the girl and the character—taught her friends how to escape boredom by entering the world of fantasy and make-believe. Sendak's illustrations richly evoke the world of 1940s Brooklyn as well as that of Rosie's vivid imagination. Years later, Rosie appeared again as the star of Sendak's half-hour animated television special, *Really Rosie, Starring the Nutshell Kids* (1975). The name Nutshell came from his acclaimed 1962 work called *The Nutshell Library,* a collection of four small books. Including one of his best-known works, *Chicken Soup with Rice, The Nutshell Library* quickly became a favorite with readers and critics and has remained popular throughout the decades since.

The Wild Things

In 1963, Sendak published the book that turned him from a well-respected author and illustrator into a world-famous, award-winning, and somewhat controversial figure. *Where the Wild Things Are* tells the story of Max, an energetic boy who gets into trouble one evening and is sent to his room without dinner. Angry with his mother, Max creates an imaginary forest out of his bedroom and escapes to a land populated by wild things. (In Sendak's original idea, the forest was filled with wild horses, but his inability to draw horses caused him to change to monsters.) The frightening monsters, with their big teeth and sharp claws, are soon tamed by Max (who becomes their king) and join him in raucous play. Eventually Max feels lonesome for home and returns to his bedroom to find a hot dinner waiting for him there. *Where the Wild Things Are* immediately took its place among children's book classics, winning the prestigious

An illustration by Maurice Sendak from The Golden Key *(1967), by George MacDonald. Picture © 1967 by Maurice Sendak. Reproduced by permission of Sunburst Books, a division of Farrar, Straus, & Giroux, LLC.*

Caldecott Medal in 1964. Some teachers and childhood experts complained, however, that Sendak's monsters were too scary for small children, with one psychologist, Bruno Bettelheim (1903–1990), claiming the book could cause psychological damage in sensitive children. Sendak responded to such criticism by saying that books like his did not introduce children to fear: such emotions are part of every child's life already, and fantasy "is the best means they have for taming Wild Things."

Sendak followed *Where the Wild Things Are* with two other enormously popular works, *In the Night Kitchen* (1970) and *Outside Over There* (1981). He considers these books a loosely connected trilogy—they do not share story lines or characters, but they do have the same themes. In the years leading up to the writing of *In the Night Kitchen,* Sendak faced several hardships: between 1967 and 1969, he suffered a heart attack, his mother and father died, and his treasured dog Jennie died. Sendak dedicated the book to his parents and made numerous private references to his dog and other loved ones in the book. *In the Night Kitchen* features a little boy named Mickey who leaves his bedroom to enter the fantasy world of the Night Kitchen. For several pages, Mickey traipses through the Night Kitchen completely nude, and several teachers and librarians objected to what they considered inappropriate drawings. Some went so far as to draw in a diaper so Mickey no longer appeared naked. For the most part, however, critics praised Sendak for his charming, comic-book-like illustrations and humorous, refreshing look into a child's fantasy life.

Sendak has described *Outside Over There* as a deeply personal book about a young girl taking care of her baby sister. (Although the baby in the book is a girl, Sendak saw a parallel between the story and the times when his sister took care of him when he was a baby.) The baby is kidnapped by goblins, and it then becomes the older sister's mission to find the baby and bring her home. With both text and pictures reaching a level of sophistication and complexity not seen before in a Sendak work, *Outside Over There* marked a milestone for Sendak: for the first time, one of his books was being marketed to both children and adults. Biographer Selma Lanes describes the book's illustrations as "more painterly, fluid, and accomplished than any previous Sendak color work."

In addition to his children's books, Sendak has also applied his considerable skills to designing costumes and sets for opera productions. A lifelong, passionate fan of music, particularly the compositions of Wolfgang Amadeus Mozart

Masterworks

1952	*A Hole Is to Dig* (illustrations)
1958	*What Do You Say, Dear?* (illustrations)
1960	*The Sign on Rosie's Door* (illustrations and text)
1962	*The Nutshell Library* (illustrations and text)
1963	*Where the Wild Things Are* (illustrations and text)
1970	*In the Night Kitchen* (illustrations and text)
1973	*The Juniper Tree and Other Tales from Grimm* (illustrations)
1981	*Outside Over There* (illustrations and text)
1999	*Swine Lake* (illustrations)

(1756–1791), Sendak rose to the challenge of "illustrating" his favorite musical works. The operas he worked on had strong elements of fantasy and held a special appeal for children. Sendak's dedication to producing quality theater for kids resulted in his co-founding the Night Kitchen Theater in 1990. Sendak's recent fiction has continued in the same vein as his early successes: he confronts the inner world of children, as well as the sometimes frightening outside world, without flinching from painful subjects. For example, *We Are All in the Dumps with Jack and Guy* (1993), Sendak's picture book based on two obscure Mother Goose rhymes, depicts poverty-stricken, homeless children. While his occasionally disturbing works have raised alarms among some critics, Sendak is generally ranked among the finest children's book illustrators and authors. Among his numerous awards are the 1970 Hans Christian Andersen International Medal (he was the first American to receive this honor) and a National Medal of the Arts, presented to him by President Bill Clinton (1946–) in 1997.

For More Information

Books

Cech, John. *Angels and Wild Things: The Archetypal Poetics of Maurice Sendak.* University Park: Pennsylvania State University Press, 1995.

Lanes, Selma G. *The Art of Maurice Sendak.* New York: Harry N. Abrams, Inc., 1980.

Web Sites

Cary, Alice. "Swine Lake: A Night at the Ballet with Maurice Sendak." *BookPage Online.* [Online] Available http://www.bookpage.com/9905bp/maurice_sendak.html (last accessed on July 5, 2001).

"The Fantasy World of Maurice Sendak." *Indianapolis Museum of Art.* [Online] Available http://www.ima-art.org/specexhibits/sendak/sendak.html (last accessed on July 5, 2001).

Long, Marion. "Maurice Sendak: A Western Canon, Jr." *HomeArts*. [Online] Available http://homearts.com/depts/relat/sendakf1.htm (last accessed on July 5, 2001).

O'Keeffe, Hope. "Maurice Sendak." *Fact Monster*. [Online] Available http://www.factmonster.com/ipka/A0801320.html (last accessed on July 5, 2001).

Cindy Sherman

Born January 19, 1954
Glen Ridge, New Jersey

American photographer

> *"Art should make people question what they take for granted in their life. Whether it has to do with gender, how they treat men or women or how they view anything. Art should make people think."*

While her medium is photography, Cindy Sherman cannot easily be classified as a photographer. She first achieved success in early 1980s New York amidst a wildly experimental era in American art. Her works, from the "Untitled Film Stills" of the late 1970s to the surreal and grotesque photographs of artificial body parts in the late 1990s, reveal a unique and sometimes disturbing vision. Rather than capturing a fleeting moment in time with her camera, Sherman carefully crafts dramatic scenes originating in her imagination—orchestrating the lighting, costumes, and makeup—and then preserves them in photographs. And in most of these "scenes," Sherman is both photographer and actor. She dresses up in an astonishing array of outfits and costumes to portray various characters that represent the way women have been depicted in films, historical artworks, and advertising. Although her message is sometimes difficult to interpret, Sherman's works offer a compelling view of the way women's roles have been defined—and sometimes restricted—by popular culture.

Playing dress-up

Born in New Jersey, Cynthia Morris Sherman was the youngest of five children growing up in suburban Long Island, New York. An imaginative child, Sherman loved movies and television, and she especially enjoyed dressing up in adult clothes and makeup, assuming the identity of an imaginary person. In an interview in *Art in America* magazine, she recalls that even as a child, she played dress-up not to make herself pretty, but to make herself look like someone else: "I would make myself up like a monster, things like that, which seemed much more fun than just looking like Barbie."

In 1972, Sherman enrolled at State University of New York (SUNY) in Buffalo to study art. She initially focused on painting, having found that she was very good at painting self-portraits and making exact copies of photographs or other paintings. She failed a photography class in her first year of college, unable to master the technical aspects of taking and developing pictures. Her next photography class, however, proved a liberating experience: the second teacher emphasized ideas over technical perfection, and Sherman began to realize the creative possibilities of photography. At the same time, she began a relationship with experimental artist Robert Longo (1953–) and started to acquaint herself with contemporary art. This exposure to the innovative ideas of other young artists made Sherman realize the importance of finding interesting concepts for her own work. She realized that the small amount of time spent making a photograph, as opposed to the time-consuming act of painting, allowed her to spend more time thinking of ideas. She abandoned the notion of becoming a painter and committed herself to photography.

In 1974, while still in college, Sherman, Longo, and a few other artists converted an old ice factory in Buffalo into a home and art gallery called Hallwalls. The following year, Sherman exhibited her first works there. Laying the groundwork for the later works that made her famous, these photographs feature Sherman as the subject, dressed in various outfits with accompanying hats and wigs. She did not merely dress up in costumes for her photographs, however; she transformed herself

Untitled Film Still, #50
(1979). Photograph by
Cindy Sherman.
*Reproduced courtesy of
Cindy Sherman and
Metro Pictures.*

into various imaginary characters much as an actress prepares for a role in a movie. In the summer of 1977, a year after graduating from college, Sherman received a fellowship (a monetary award in recognition of her accomplishments) from the National Endowment of the Arts. She moved to New York City with Longo and spent the next three years creating her first major series of photographs, called "Untitled Film Stills."

A star in the New York art world

Sherman's "Untitled Film Stills" had a swift and powerful impact on the American art scene, marking the beginning of her rapid rise from unknown artist to celebrity. Consisting of sixty-nine black-and-white photographs, this series features Sherman as the subject in every image. Each of these imaginary "film stills" portrays a character that might have appeared in a 1950s movie (film stills are photographs, as opposed to moving pictures, taken of a scene in a movie). The photos do not portray Sherman as specific actresses or characters, but as general character types, such as an innocent girl making her way in the big city, a sophisticated modern woman, and a vulnerable yet sexy blonde bombshell. While the pictures feature Sherman as the subject, they could not be accurately described as self-portraits. In fact, Sherman disguises herself so thoroughly in the characters she portrays that she is frequently unrecognizable.

Critics have debated whether Sherman's "Untitled Film Stills" poke fun at or reinforce traditional, and sometimes negative, images of women. The artist herself has offered minimal insight, preferring to let audiences and scholars interpret her works' meaning. She has said that these photographs reflect the tension that results from growing up female in a society that encourages girls to behave in a ladylike way while also projecting images of women—in advertising and films—as glamorous and seductive. Her reluctance to speak about her art, as well as the fact that none of her pictures has a title beyond a number (*Untitled Film Still #13,* for example), lends a mysterious, intriguing aspect to her work. Sherman's role as model for these pictures means that for many of the shots, someone else actually took the picture (for some, the photographer used a remote device to trigger the shutter). Challenging the strict definition of photographer, Sherman created a complete dramatic work with each picture, generating the idea, designing the set, costume, and makeup, and acting as the character. She has resisted the label of photographer, preferring instead the more general description of an artist who works in photography.

In 1980, Sherman created her first series of color photographs. Continuing her exploration of the artificial world of movies, Sherman, again using herself as the model, portrayed various characters, each set against a false backdrop. She used slide projections—mainly images of city streets—as the background for her characters, making it look as though the photographs were shot "on location," when really she never had to leave her studio. Her next major series, what Peter Schjeldahl in *Cindy Sherman* describes as "her first fully mature work," had its inspiration in the centerfolds of pornographic magazines. While the women in this 1981 series (again, all portrayed by Sherman) are fully clothed, they do have a vulnerable quality that makes them seem exposed. In most of these pictures, the women are lying down and the camera is positioned above them, enhancing the women's solitude and defenselessness. Their eyes, staring at a fixed point in space, give these photographs an eerie, hypnotic quality. Remarking on the critical reaction to this series, Schjeldahl recalls that the images "were an art world smash which quickly assumed international proportions." In another highly successful color series in 1983, Sherman borrowed costumes from a fashion designer and again explored various types of theatrical roles played by women.

A new direction

Throughout the 1980s, Sherman had more than thirty solo shows at important galleries and museums around the world. A shy, private person, Sherman was uncomfortable with her rapid success and newfound fame. After her initial success, Sherman sought new ways to explore the medium of photography. As a follow-up to the charm and seductiveness of many of the "Untitled Film Stills," she began exploring the darker, seamier side of physical beauty. She was hired to shoot a series of fashion photographs for *Interview* magazine, and for that project Sherman ignored traditional notions of beauty and glamour, opting instead for what she called "happy, goofy, funny" pictures of herself in high-fashion clothing. For subsequent commissions, Sherman further upset fashion conventions by dressing in beautiful clothes and then making herself up to look gruesome. Using makeup, she created scars and bruises for her face, and she attached artificial limbs to her body.

In the mid-1980s, Sherman explored the world of fairy tales in her photographs. Examining the dark and frightening side of the genre, Sherman dressed in elaborate costumes and made herself hideous with makeup effects such as warts, horns, and fake noses. She used costumes again in the late 1980s for a series generally referred to as the "history portraits," in which she dressed as both real and fictional people as they had been portrayed by the world's great artists. For example, in *Untitled #204,* Sherman imitates a painting by **Jean-Auguste-Dominique Ingres** (pronounced ANG-ruh, 1780–1867; see entry in volume 3) called *Marie-Clothilde-Ines de Foucauld, Madame Moitessier* (1851). In Ingres's portrait, the subject is an elegant lady wearing fine clothes and expensive jewelry. Sherman's photograph, while bearing a resemblance to the Ingres painting, shows a woman whose face is bruised and whose clothes and jewelry are plain and time-worn. Sherman's photograph draws attention to the contrast between idealized, classical portraits of women and the harsher reality that many women actually face.

The artificial body parts that Sherman first used in her fashion photography became a feature in many of her subsequent series. She used both realistic devices obtained from medical supply companies as well as parts from plastic dolls and mannequins. Depicting grotesquely twisted and mutilated body parts, Sherman created bizarre scenes of violence and disaster. Her use of lighting, makeup, and special effects made the images realistically horrifying, but the use of obviously fake body parts offset their gruesomeness; the resulting images are disturbing while also being humorous. These photographs are notable exceptions to Sherman's previous work in that she does not "star" in them; while Sherman's face does appear in some of these pictures, many of them consist completely of doll and mannequin parts. Her fascination with horror and violence found a new expression in 1997: Sherman directed a feature film called *Office Killer,* in which a woman accidentally kills one of her coworkers and then goes on a violent rampage. The character takes her victims' bodies back to her apartment to arrange them in scenes of an ideal office, a practice not unlike Sherman's photographs in which she arranges plastic body parts into gory episodes.

Masterworks

1978	*Untitled Film Still #7*
	Untitled Film Still #13
1979	*Untitled Film Still #48*
1980	*Untitled Film Still #54*
1981	*Untitled #96*
1983	*Untitled #119*
	Untitled #123
1985	*Untitled #153*
1989	*Untitled #188*
1994	*Untitled #211*
	Untitled #302

The success that came so quickly to Cindy Sherman has continued over the two decades of her career. Retrospective exhibits of her works have been featured at many of the world's most significant museums. In 1995, the Museum of Modern Art in New York purchased the entire "Untitled Film Stills" series for more than $1 million. That same year, she earned a MacArthur Foundation "genius" grant, a prestigious and financially lucrative award. Described by many as a conceptual, or idea-driven, artist rather than a photographer, Sherman has brought tremendous creativity to her various series of photographs, exploring one intriguing idea after another. In an essay in the book *Cindy Sherman,* I. Michael Danoff praises her unique talent: "She has the courage and the drive to experiment and to challenge her abilities. She resists the ease of allowing a concept to linger and weaken. She seems to search, mine, and move on."

For More Information

Books and Periodicals

Cruz, Amanda. *Cindy Sherman: Retrospective.* New York: Thames and Hudson, 2000.

Fuku, Noriko. "A Woman of Parts." *Art in America* 85 (June 1997): p. 74.

Miller, Barbara L. "Sherman's Mass Appeal." *Afterimage* 25 (November–December 1997): p. 5.

Sherman, Cindy. *Cindy Sherman.* New York: Pantheon Books, 1984.

Sills, Leslie. *In Real Life: Six Women Photographers.* New York: Holiday House, 2000.

Web Sites

"Cindy Sherman Study Modules." *Art Gallery of Ontario.* [Online] Available http://www.ago.on.ca/information/exhibitions/modules/sherman/main_frame.html (last accessed on July 5, 2001).

"The Complete *Untitled Film Stills:* Cindy Sherman." *Museum of Modern Art.* [Online] Available http://www.moma.org/exhibitions/sherman/ (last accessed on July 5, 2001).

Helfand, Glen. "Cindy Sherman: From Dream Girl to Nightmare Alley." *Salon.* [Online] Available http://www. salon.com/media/1997/12/08media.html (last accessed on July 5, 2001).

Papagiannis, Helen. "Cindy Sherman." *Masters of Photography.* [Online] Available http://www.masters-of-photography.com/S/sherman/sherman.html (last accessed on July 5, 2001).

Papagiannis, Helen. *Cindy Sherman's Masquerade.* [Online] Available http://citd.scar.utoronto.ca/VPAB04/projects/Helen_Papagiannis/home.htm (last accessed on July 5, 2001).

Louis Comfort Tiffany

Born February 18, 1848
New York, New York

Died January 17, 1933
New York, New York

American painter, craftsman,
decorator, and designer

"What is the Quest of Beauty? What else is the goal that an artist sets before him, but that same spirit of beauty!"

▲ *Louis Comfort Tiffany.*
Photograph, Museum of the City of New York. Reproduced by permission of Archive Photos.

Known today primarily for his colorful, intricately designed stained-glass lamps, Louis Comfort Tiffany forged a long and successful artistic career, delving into many branches of the decorative arts. Mainly a designer of glassware, Tiffany also produced metalwork, jewelry, furniture, and ceramics. He described his artistic mission as a desire to create beautiful objects and make them accessible to as many people as possible. He wished to raise the standard for interior design and for such household necessities as lamps and glassware, producing items that were attractive and unique as well as functional. Tiffany felt that the decorative arts should have the same status as fine arts, such as painting and sculpture.

As a young man, he was impressed by the ideals of the arts and crafts movement in England. This movement, reacting against the mass-production techniques of the Industrial Revolution (which began in England in the mid-1700s and continued through the mid-1800s), advocated a return to simplicity and to handmade, rather than machine-made, crafts. The arts and crafts movement laid the groundwork for the art nouveau movement, which flourished between about 1890 and 1910. Art nouveau, primarily found in architecture, interior design, jewelry, and illustration, was usually characterized by the curving, graceful lines of nature: flower stalks, vines, and insect wings. Tiffany became a leading proponent of the art nouveau movement in the United States, transferring his love of nature and his passion for light and color to the creation of his signature lampshades and glassware. As the leader of a promising business, he later parted ways with the arts and crafts movement by instituting mass-production techniques, though still ensuring that his merchandise retained the look and feel of hand-crafted items.

A privileged life

Louis Comfort Tiffany was born into a wealthy family that could trace its American ancestors back to the 1600s. His father, Charles Lewis Tiffany, was the founder and director of the famed Tiffany and Company jewelry store; his mother, Harriet Olivia Tiffany, was the sister of Charles's first business partner, John Young. Louis Tiffany grew up in a life of privilege, with the expectation that he would take over the family business as an adult. But he had other plans: he wanted to be a painter. After graduating from high school, Tiffany studied painting as an apprentice to landscape artist George Inness (1825–1894). Tiffany then moved to Paris to study with Leon Bailly, after which he spent some time traveling throughout Europe and North Africa. He captured scenes of his travels in his oil and watercolor paintings, and upon his return to New York in 1870, exhibited his works with some success.

Tiffany married Mary Woodbridge Goddard in May 1872; together, they had four children—two sons and two daughters. While he continued to paint throughout his life, Tiffany gradually became more and more involved in a design career. His family connections meant that he had many acquaintances among the wealthy and powerful, and he began applying his artistic sensibilities to designing their homes. With some of his colleagues,

The Arts and Crafts Movement

"Have nothing in your houses that you do not know to be useful, or believe to be beautiful," urged William Morris (1834–1896), the founder and chief advocate of the arts and crafts movement. This movement arose in England as a reaction to what many believed were the dehumanizing effects of the Industrial Revolution, which marked the transition from handmade goods to those produced in a factory. Sticking with methods that had been in existence for hundreds of years, Morris and his associates designed wallpaper, furniture, jewelry, and, with the founding of Kelmscott Press, books.

Morris believed that reverting to traditional arts would benefit the working classes, but the merchandise he produced turned out to be too expensive for the average family. Nevertheless, his commitment to handmade crafts endured in the work of artists and designers who read his writings and agreed with his ideas. One of the most important figures who built on Morris's example was Scottish architect Charles Rennie Mackintosh (1868–1924), whose tearooms in Glasgow are acknowledged as design masterpieces. The arts and crafts movement had particular appeal in America, notably upon architect Frank Lloyd Wright (1867–1959; see entry in volume 2), stained-glass artist Louis Comfort Tiffany, and furniture maker Gustave Stickley (1858–1942). In the era of the Internet, Morris's ideals live on at the Arts & Crafts Society's website, available at http://www.arts-crafts.com.

Tiffany formed a decorating firm in 1879 called Louis C. Tiffany and Associated Artists. They had many famous and wealthy clients, including author Mark Twain (1835–1910) and industrialist Cornelius Vanderbilt (1843–1899). Tiffany and his company rose to such eminence in this field that they were offered a commission to design several rooms of the White House in 1883, during the presidency of Chester A. Arthur (1829–1886). Associated Artists also designed public and religious buildings, including libraries, theaters, and churches.

Turns to glassmaking

Tiffany had studied glassmaking at the Heidt glassworks in Brooklyn in the 1870s, and eventually his passion for that craft surpassed his interest in home decorating. While he continued working in interior design for many years after, he broke off from Associated Artists to spend more time on glasswork in 1883. Unsatisfied with commonly used methods for coloring glass, such as painting the glass's surface and then burning the color onto the glass, Tiffany developed an innovative technique that injected colors in various combinations directly into the molten glass. Working with chemists, Tiffany was able to achieve a wide range of lustrous, vibrant colors. His push for innovation in blown glass eventually led to the development of the iridescent, richly colored glass Tiffany trademarked as Favrile, explaining in a brochure from 1896 that the name comes from an Old English word meaning "belonging to a craftsman or his craft."

Water lily lamp (c. 1910). Designed by Louis Comfort Tiffany. Reproduced by permission of the Corbis Corporation.

In 1884, after twelve years of marriage, Tiffany's wife Mary died. His grief over his wife's death, combined with some business troubles, made for a difficult period in Tiffany's life. He continued to change the direction of his business, forming the Tiffany Glass Company in 1885. He also rebuilt his personal life, marrying Louise Wakeman Knox in 1886. At first, his company continued in the interior design arena, while also assembling stained-glass windows. Eventually, however, the Tiffany Glass Company (its name changed to Tiffany Glass and Decorating Company in 1892) became the springboard for Tiffany's greatest period of innovation and glass production.

A trip to Paris for the International Exhibition in 1889 exposed Tiffany to some of the inventive techniques in blown glass that had been developed by Europe's top designers. A few years later, after much experimentation, Tiffany and his team of chemists, designers, and glass workers had come up with several unique designs and innovative effects of their own, resulting in the vases, tiles, and other glassware that made Tiffany a household name. Characterized by the wide range of

Jack-in-the-Pulpit Vase (c. 1912). Designed by Louis Comfort Tiffany. Photograph, © James L. Amos. Reproduced by permission of the Corbis Corporation.

shimmering colors, some Tiffany glasswares were also remarkable for their unusual textures. Cypriote glass, for example, had a rough, ancient-looking texture that was achieved by rolling the object in crumbled bits of glass. Lava glass, another Tiffany specialty, was created to look like hardened volcanic lava.

While several scholars note that his vases and other glassware mark his highest artistic achievement, Tiffany is perhaps best known for his stained (also called leaded) glass. Whether in the form of large, impressive windows or smaller-scale works such as his lampshades, leaded glass allowed Tiffany to express his passion for color, light, and the beauty found in nature. By itself, Tiffany's glass had a rich, deep color; when light streamed through his windows, the bits of glass glowed like jewels. Over the years, Tiffany created numerous leaded-glass works for home decoration, and he also received commissions from churches for his windows. Unlike the traditional church stained glass that depicts biblical scenes, Tiffany's windows display his reverence for nature. His largest work of this type was a glass curtain for the National Theater in Mexico City, Mexico, that weighed several tons and consisted of two hundred panels.

The rise, fall, and rediscovery of Tiffany glass

By the end of the 1800s, Tiffany products were wildly popular; no well-decorated home could be without at least one Tiffany item. Striving to accommodate both the high public demand for his products and his desire to retain the quality of work done by master craftsmen, Tiffany set up huge workshops, employing glassmaking experts and large teams of well-trained assistants. In 1900, changing the name of the company again, this time to Tiffany Studios, Tiffany began selling his famous lamps. The lamps usually consisted of a bronze base beneath a colorful leaded-glass shade, usually done in a floral design. The demand for Tiffany lamps was so high that the methods for producing them had to change. While still designed by experts under the close supervision of Tiffany, many of the lamps were produced on assembly lines. His critics complained that Tiffany had sold out the ideals of quality craftsmanship to attain commercial success. Many observers have noted, however, that Tiffany's company actually lost money in the production of stained glass, and Tiffany kept his company afloat through infusions of cash from his personal fortune. In any case, experts have noted that little difference could be seen between the hand-crafted stained-glass items and the mass-produced ones. By producing his products in such large quantities, Tiffany fulfilled his goal of making attractive household art more affordable for the buying public. For moderate sums of money, consumers could own works that closely resembled the handmade versions that were shown in museums and won prizes at international expositions.

At the peak of his success, Tiffany decided to take on one more top-to-bottom home design: that of his own estate, built on a large piece of land in Oyster Bay, an area of New York's Long Island. Completed in 1904, Laurelton Hall was conceived as more than just a home—the estate included a museum, an art studio and school, and a retreat for artists. Tiffany intended the compound to be a lasting legacy of his artistic vision, and he endowed a large sum of money to maintain a foundation and support artist scholarships. But money troubles in the decades after his death led to the sale of the home's contents and eventually of the land and the house itself. In 1957, Laurelton Hall was nearly destroyed by a fire.

In the last years of his life, Tiffany's work declined in popularity, and suddenly the once-coveted Tiffany originals were gathering dust in a warehouse. For two decades after his death in 1933, Tiffany's decorative style was out of step with American design fashion, but the 1950s saw a revival of his work. A retrospective exhibit of his work in 1958 and an art nouveau show at New York's Museum of Modern Art in 1960 marked a renewed appreciation for Tiffany's artistic vision and unique talents. In fact, original Tiffany lamps became so highly prized among collectors in the latter half of the twentieth century that their prices rose to astronomical heights, in a direct reversal of the artist's original intention to make his works of art affordable to the masses. At a 1998 auction, two Tiffany lamps fetched some of the highest auction prices for decorative items in U.S. history, selling for nearly two million dollars each.

For More Information

Books

Duncan, Alastair. *The Masterworks of Louis Comfort Tiffany.* New York: Abradale Press, 1993.

Koch, Robert. *Louis C. Tiffany, Rebel in Glass.* New York: Crown Publishers, 1982.

Paul, Tessa. *The Art of Louis Comfort Tiffany.* New York: Exeter Books, 1987.

Web Sites

"Louis Comfort Tiffany." *Charles Hosmer Morse Museum of American Art.* [Online] Available http://www.morsemuseum.org/louis.html (last accessed on June 8, 2001).

"Louis Comfort Tiffany." *The Metropolitan Museum of Art.* [Online] Available http://www.metmuseum.org/explore/Tiffany/RELEASE.HTM (last accessed on June 8, 2001).

Schuldenfrei, Robin S. "Louis Comfort Tiffany: An American Entrepreneur." [Online] Available http://www.tiac.net/users/tangaroa/tc2.html (last accessed on June 8, 2001).

Jan Vermeer

Born October 1632
Delft, Netherlands
Died December 1675
Delft, Netherlands

Dutch painter

Whether depicting the everyday world of working people or the elegant clothing and genteel surroundings of wealthy aristocrats, Jan Vermeer's paintings offer a vivid picture of life in a Dutch city of the distant past. But while he chose everyday subjects, Vermeer would not be described as a realist. Unlike some of his contemporaries, who wished to portray their world as it really appeared, flaws and all, Vermeer tended to idealize his subjects, creating scenes of quiet contemplation, beautifully lit by sunlight streaming through windows. His best-known works depict women absorbed in their work or recreation, dressed in rich colors and bathed in soft light. Vermeer's approach to the design of his pictures was scientific in its precision, resulting in expertly composed works. With a relatively small body of work credited to him—only around thirty-five paintings—Vermeer is hailed as a master artist of the Golden Age of Dutch painting.

"Nothing else in art even remotely resembles the glinting, shivering surfaces that Vermeer gives to all sorts of substances. . . ."

Jed Perl, "Mystery Master"

At a time when their European neighbors were embroiled in the Thirty Years' War (1618–48), the Dutch people enjoyed a period of great prosperity and cultural riches known as the Golden Age. The Netherlands' northern provinces obtained independence from Spain (and consequently, from the Catholic Church) in the early 1600s, and the birth of the Dutch nation coincided with a flowering of Dutch art that lasted for much of the century. Artists were freed from the tradition of painting grand religious subjects and focused instead on the smaller details of everyday life. Vermeer, who married into a Catholic family, painted a few religious works, but his best-known paintings intimately capture the lives of his fellow Dutch citizens.

An obscured life

Few records exist documenting the life of Jan (also known as Johannes) Vermeer (pronounced YON ver-MARE). He was born—and indeed lived his whole life—in Delft, where his parents, Reynier and Digna Vermeer, owned a tavern. His father was also an art dealer, and many historians have speculated that the younger Vermeer made his living that way as well. In 1653, Vermeer married Catharina Bolnes. The couple had fifteen children, four of whom died early on. In the same year as his marriage, Vermeer entered the Guild of Saint Luke, an artist's guild, as a master painter. A guild is an association designed to promote a certain profession, whether a business or an artistic pursuit. To earn the title of master painter, Vermeer would have had to train with other guild members, eventually producing a work of his own that could be described as a masterpiece. Vermeer served as the head of his guild twice, once in 1662 and again in 1670.

Records indicate that Vermeer established a reputation as a master beyond his native country, and he appears to have sold a few of his works during his lifetime. But he must have had another form of income to support his large family; he probably sold the artworks of others. Even so, the Vermeer family struggled financially, and the artist's death at the age of forty-three left his wife responsible for paying debts and raising eleven

children. After his death, Vermeer was all but forgotten and his few dozen paintings were attributed to other artists until nearly two hundred years later. In 1842, art historian Théophile Thoré (also known as W. Bürger) came across the painting *A View of Delft*. This work thrilled him, and Thoré spent twenty years of his life researching the true identity of its painter. In 1866, he published a book revealing that this picture, along with more than sixty others, had been painted by Vermeer. Scholars have since narrowed the total number of Vermeer paintings to around thirty-five. The difficulty of determining which paintings were actually Vermeers has been enhanced by numerous forgery

View of Delft (1658–60).
Painting by Jan Vermeer.
Oil on canvas. 96.5 x
115.7 cm (38 x 45⁵⁄₁₆ in).
Photograph, The Art
Archive/Mauritshuis
Hague/Album/Joseph
Martin. Reproduced
by permission.

attempts, notably those of Hans van Meegeren (1889–1947) in the middle of the twentieth century. Because of the scarcity of records left by Vermeer, and because only a few of his works are dated, historians have also had a great deal of trouble determining the chronology of his paintings.

Life in Delft

Though he is best known for his works portraying contemporary life, some of Vermeer's earlier works covered broad historical and religious themes. His religious painting *Christ in the House of Mary and Martha* and the mythological *Diana and Her Companions* indicate the attempts of a young artist to find his own style and technique while painting traditional subjects. Although the content, colors, and style of these early works are quite different from Vermeer's mature paintings, the mood—thoughtful, quiet, and peaceful—remains the same. By the late 1650s, when Vermeer was around twenty-five years old, he had developed his own style and settled on his favorite subjects, which would result in the works for which he is best known.

Beginning with such paintings as *Girl Reading a Letter at an Open Window* (c. 1657), Vermeer painted a number of works showing women involved in so-called traditional feminine activities: reading and writing letters, doing domestic chores, playing musical instruments, socializing with gentlemen callers. In many of these pictures, a woman is standing alone, to the right of an open window, warmly lit by the sun and completely absorbed in her task. In *The Milkmaid,* one of Vermeer's most famous images, a woman stands at a table pouring milk from a jug. She is dressed in rich gold and red with a deep blue apron. Her look of serene concentration gives the viewer a sense of glimpsing a private moment; this intimate mood pervades most of Vermeer's paintings.

Several of Vermeer's pictures of women depict more complex and mysterious scenes, showing the subjects—through the reading of letters or interactions with men—involved in subtle, complicated relationships. In *The Concert,* two women and a man sit at a piano. The tone of the relationship between the two women and the man is unclear. The

The Concert (c. 1665–66). Painting by Jan Vermeer. Oil on canvas. 28½ x 25½ in (72.5 x 64.7 cm). Isabella Stewart Gardner Museum, Boston. Photograph reproduced by permission of the Granger Collection.

man's back is to the viewer, so his face offers no clues, and the women seem engrossed in their musical performance. Music as a metaphor for seduction was a common theme in Dutch painting at the time, and one of the pictures that hangs on the wall behind the piano depicts a scene of sexual promiscuity. The figures in Vermeer's painting, however, seem earnestly absorbed in their music, perhaps suggesting an innocent contrast to the picture hanging behind them.

Most of Vermeer's paintings take place indoors, but he painted two landscapes of his native Delft that rank among his best works. *Little Street,* as the name implies, shows a small section of a cobblestone street, though the real subjects of the painting are the few buildings and people across the street. Within a small area—the painting measures only around twenty-one by seventeen inches—Vermeer has captured the tranquil charm of his community. A woman sits sewing in an open doorway while another stands in a passageway leading to

Inspiring Art

Great art has inspired countless works of poetry, drama, music, and fiction. One of the best-known works of English poet John Keats (1795–1821) is "Ode on a Grecian Urn," a poem inspired by a piece of ancient pottery. Anglo-American author W. H. Auden (1907–1973) based his poem "Musée des Beaux Arts" on a painting called *Landscape with the Fall of Icarus* (c. 1558) by Flemish landscape painter Pieter Bruegel (1525–1569). American composer Gunther Schuller (1925–) was sparked by the artworks of **Paul Klee** (1879–1940; see entry in volume 3) when he wrote his orchestral work *Seven Studies on Themes of Paul Klee* (1959). And the Broadway musical *Sunday in the Park with George* (1984) by Stephen Sondheim (1930–) was based on the masterpiece *A Sunday Afternoon on the Island of La Grande Jatte* (1884–86) by French painter Georges Seurat (1859–1891; see entry in volume 2).

In recent years, one artist's works have inspired several works of literature. The paintings of Jan Vermeer—quiet, peaceful, and mysterious—have ignited the imaginations of millions of viewers over the centuries, and at the turn of the twenty-first century three novelists chose Vermeer paintings—real and imaginary—as the subjects of their books. Perhaps because so little is known about Vermeer and the women he painted, these authors felt drawn to fill in the gaps with stories from their imaginations.

In *Girl with a Pearl Earring* (1999), Tracy Chevalier tells the story of Griet, a young woman who works for the Vermeer family and is given the important task of cleaning the artist's studio. Griet eventually models for Vermeer, resulting in the work of the book's title. The real story behind the painting, one of Vermeer's most famous, is unknown. For *Girl in Hyacinth Blue* (1999), Susan Vreeland imagined not just the details surrounding a Vermeer painting's creation but also the painting itself. Going backward in time from present day to Vermeer's lifetime, each chapter of the book tells a different story with the fictional painting at its center. Another imaginary Vermeer painting (though with the same title as a real work) is at the heart of *The Music Lesson* (2000) by Katharine Weber. In this work, an art historian becomes involved with the theft of a Vermeer painting held for ransom by a splinter group of the Irish Republican Army (IRA), a controversial paramilitary organization fighting for independence from Britain in Northern Ireland.

an unseen courtyard. Two children kneel on the sidewalk, absorbed in a game. Placed amongst the textured brick facades of the buildings, the people give a sense of what Arthur Wheelock, in the book *Johannes Vermeer*, described as "the poetic beauty of everyday life." While *Little Street* has a universal quality, Vermeer's other landscape, *View of Delft*, belongs to a specific time and place. Much larger in scale than *Little Street*, *View of Delft* has a dramatic quality that is somewhat lost in reproductions. It was this painting that inspired nineteenth-century historian Thoré to uncover all of Vermeer's surviving works, and *View of Delft* occupies a position of importance in the masterwork of French novelist Marcel Proust (PROOST; 1871–1922), *Remembrance of Things Past*.

A technical approach

While widely acknowledged as a master of light and color, Vermeer is not considered a great draftsman, particularly in his drawings of the human body. While pointing out imprecision and imperfections in his lines, though, art critics describe the overall composition of Vermeer's works as masterful. His paintings of interiors show a preoccupation with the placement of figures and objects within a defined space. His works also indicate an interest in optics, the science of vision and light. Most scholars assume that Vermeer experimented with the camera obscura, a precursor to the modern camera that used a lens and mirrors to project images onto a viewing screen. An image from a camera obscura would show exaggerated perspective and tricks of light that the human eye ordinarily would not perceive. Such elements show up in many of Vermeer's paintings. In *A Lady at the Virginals with a Gentleman* (also called *The Music Lesson*; "virginals" refers to a piano-like instrument popular in Vermeer's time), the depth of the room is indicated in part by the black and white floor tiles that decrease in size from the front of the room to the back, and by the large table in the foreground compared to the smaller figures in the background. In numerous Vermeer paintings, like the widely admired *Girl with a Pearl Earring*, the unique properties of light are shown in the glistening highlights of a pearl earring, a woman's skin, a gold-

Masterworks

c. 1657   *A Girl Asleep*

            Girl Reading a Letter at an Open Window

c. 1657–58 *The Little Street*

c. 1658–60 *The Milkmaid* (also called *The Kitchen Maid*)

c. 1660–61 *View of Delft*

c. 1662–64 *A Lady at the Virginals with a Gentleman* (also called *The Music Lesson*)

c. 1664   *Woman Holding a Balance*

c. 1664–65 *Young Woman with a Water Pitcher*

c. 1665–66 *Girl with a Pearl Earring*

c. 1666–67 *The Allegory of Painting* (also called *The Art of Painting*)

c. 1669–70 *The Lacemaker*

en shawl. While Vermeer's technical experiments and contemporary subject matter were rooted in his time and place, his surviving works continue to exert a timeless appeal.

For More Information

Books and Periodicals

Brusati, Celeste. *Johannes Vermeer.* New York: Rizzoli International Publications, 1993.

Perl, Jed. "Mystery Master." *The New Republic* 214 (January 8, 1996): p. 35.

Sweet, Christopher. *The Essential Johannes Vermeer.* Kansas City, MO: Andrews McMeel Publishing, 1999.

Wheelock, Arthur K., Jr. *Johannes Vermeer.* New Haven and London: Yale University Press, 1995.

Wheelock, Arthur K., Jr. *Vermeer: The Complete Works.* New York: Harry N. Abrams, Inc., 1997.

Web Sites

"Jan Vermeer." *Mark Harden's Artchive.* [Online] Available http://artchive.com/artchive/V/vermeer.html (last accessed on July 5, 2001).

"Jan Vermeer." *World Art Treasures: Jacques-Edouard Berger Foundation.* [Online] Available http://www.bergerfoundation.ch/wat4/museum?museum=Vermeer&cd=6316-3031-3939:6316-3031-3938 (last accessed on July 5, 2001).

"Tour: Johannes Vermeer and Dutch Scenes of Daily Life in the 1600s." *National Gallery of Art, USA.* [Online] Available http://www.nga.gov/collection/gallery/gg51/gg51-main1.html (last accessed on July 5, 2001).

"Vermeer." *CGFA*. [Online] Available http://sunsite.auc.dk/ cgfa/vermeer/ (last accessed on July 5, 2001).

"Vermeer, Jan." *WebMuseum, Paris.* [Online] Available http:// www.ibiblio.org/wm/paint/auth/vermeer/ (last accessed on July 5, 2001).

James Whistler

Born July 11, 1834
Lowell, Massachusetts

Died July 17, 1903
London, England

Painter, etcher, and interior designer

▲ *James Whistler. Reproduced by permission of Archive Photos.*

James Whistler is best known for painting *Arrangement in Grey and Black: Portrait of the Painter's Mother* (1871), often called "Whistler's Mother." His place in the history of modern art, however, stems from much more than this singular masterpiece. Whistler fiercely defended the idea that, rather than teach a moral lesson, art only needs to please the eye, and his body of work supports this position by presenting numerous ways in which the harmony of colors and forms stands as its own reward.

Whistler led a very public life, and he used his celebrity to spread his unconventional views. This attitude led to one of the most remarkable episodes in nineteenth-century art—he sued art critic John Ruskin (1819–1900) for something he wrote about one of his pictures, and the media outcry that followed provoked discussion throughout Europe and America on the topic of aesthetics, or the qualities that make a work of art beautiful. Instead of merely signing his pictures, he created a butterfly insignia. Always eager to provoke those he considered closed-minded, Whistler wrote a book about his confrontational manner, titled *The Gentle Art of Making Enemies.*

America, Russia, England, and back again

It is noteworthy that while James Whistler eventually sought fame in Europe, his background was strongly American. John Whistler, the artist's grandfather, fought in the Revolutionary War and the War of 1812, and his father was named George Washington Whistler after the nation's first president. George Washington Whistler's marriage to Anna McNeill was his second. He was a widower and the father of three children when they met. James Abbott McNeill Whistler was the first of his parents' five children—all boys.

George Washington Whistler was a civil engineer who specialized in the construction of railroad lines. In 1842, he was hired to build a railroad connecting Moscow and St. Petersburg, and the family followed him to Russia. At the age of thirteen, James Whistler—known as "Jimmie"—developed rheumatic fever, a condition that required him to stay in bed for long periods. To occupy his mind, his sister Deborah gave him a book of engravings by English artist William Hogarth (1697–1764), considered one of the masters of satire. Hogarth's sense of humor appealed to Whistler as much as his drawing style, and he began to imitate him. To facilitate his recovery, the boy was sent to England, where he attended boarding school in Bristol and stayed with Deborah, who was now married to a Londoner named Francis Haden. During this time, Whistler's father fell victim to the cholera epidemic that was then sweeping through Russia, and upon his death in 1849 the family returned to America. It is clear that the European experiences of the budding young artist had a permanent impact on the way his career would unfold. He always felt more at home in Europe than in his homeland.

In 1851, Whistler was enrolled in the Military Academy at West Point; the rules had to be bent to admit a candidate who was only five feet, four inches tall, and had extremely poor vision. The discipline imposed at the Academy did not agree with Whistler, who already wanted to become an artist despite his mother's wish that he pursue a career either in the ministry or else as an engineer like his father. He was discharged from the Academy after three years.

Follows his dream to Paris

A popular novel of the day, *Scènes de la vie de Bohème* (*Scenes of Bohemian Living*), by Henri Murger (1822–1861), depicted the impoverished but romantic life of "bohemians"— artistic rebels— in the Latin Quarter of Paris, and when Whistler read it he became determined to carve out a similar existence. In November 1855, at twenty-one years of age, he set out for Paris. He lived off an allowance from home and the money he made by pawning his clothing and other possessions. Whistler enrolled in studio art classes but often failed to show up, explaining that he had overslept. To his new friends, Whistler seemed to do very little work. In private, however, he maintained a rigid work schedule.

Whistler's favorite artists were Dutchman **Rembrandt van Rijn** (1606–1669; see entry in volume 2 and update in volume 4) and Spaniard Diego Velázquez (1599–1660; see entry in volume 2), both seventeenth-century painters with many works hanging in the Louvre museum, as well as Gustave Courbet (1819–1877), who was beginning to stir up controversy in the Paris art world. Rejected by the official art expositions, Courbet mounted his own exhibitions to compete with what he considered to be stale reworkings of the past. Whistler befriended this rebellious figure and imitated the way he applied paint to canvas—in an energetic but never sloppy manner.

It was during one of Whistler's many trips to London to visit his sister that he completed his first noteworthy painting. *At the Piano* (1858–59) shows Deborah and her daughter in a simple yet elegant setting. Deborah's stately posture and long black dress anticipate the pose their mother would assume in *Arrangement in Grey and Black.* *The White Girl* followed in 1862; this painting featured the artist's girlfriend, Joanna Hiffernan, in a loose gown. Because women did not normally

appear in public dressed this way, *The White Girl* caused a small scandal, and from this point on, controversy remained a steady part of Whistler's career.

Symphonies and scandal

Rather than the solid forms and earthy colors of his mentor Courbet, *The White Girl* reflected Whistler's interest in how women appeared in the paintings of the English pre-Raphaelites. The pre-Raphaelite brotherhood was a group of

Arrangement in Grey and Black: Portrait of the Painter's Mother. *Popularly known as "Whistler's Mother" (1871). Painting by James Whistler. Oil on canvas. 56¾ x 64 in (144.3 x 162.5 cm).* Musée d'Orsay, Paris. Photograph reproduced by permission of the Corbis Corporation.

English artists, who, although inspired by religious paintings of the early Renaissance, created distinctly nonreligious artworks. The pre-Raphaelites advocated moral behavior that defied the prevailing notions of what was appropriate, and Whistler was attracted to their rebelliousness as much as he was to their art. Whistler's association with Dante Gabriel Rossetti (1828–1882), Algernon Charles Swinburne (1837–1909), and other pre-Raphaelite poets and painters brought him into conflict with Francis and Deborah Haden.

Family tensions increased in 1863, when Whistler's mother relocated to London to escape the confusion of the American Civil War (1861–65). Whistler was living with but not married to Joanna Hiffernan, and Anna Whistler would not have approved, so Hiffernan had to move out for a time. Although Whistler purposely selected a title for his mother's portrait that would emphasize color as the most important element, *Arrangement in Grey and Black* betrays some of the mixed emotions he felt for the sitter. It is perhaps these emotions that have made the painting such an enduring symbol of motherhood.

The relationship between art and music intrigued Whistler and led him to retitle *The White Girl* as *Symphony in White, No. 1.* A subsequent work titled *Symphony in White, No. 3* exasperated a critic who commented on the other colors in the painting, such as the red hair of one model, the brown hair of the other. Whistler penned an angry response, asking, "Did this person expect white hair and chalked faces? And does he then, in his astounding ignorance, believe that a symphony in F contains no other note, but shall be a continual repetition of F.F.F. . . . Fool!" This episode was but a small battle compared to the war he later fought with John Ruskin.

This war would be fought over one of his *Nocturne* paintings, a term also taken from the musical world. Frédéric Chopin (1810–1849) and later Claude Debussy (1862–1918) specialized in these compositions meant to be performed after dark, and Whistler sought after the same dreamy and atmospheric quality. He painted *Nocturne in Blue and Gold:*

Valparaiso in the South American country of Chile in 1866. He continued to work on these nighttime scenes on and off for the next fifteen years. *Nocturne in Black and Gold: The Falling Rocket,* from about 1875, provoked Ruskin to write, "I have seen, and heard, much of Cockney impudence before now; but never expected to hear a coxcomb ask two hundred guineas for flinging a pot of paint in the public's face."

Ruskin, the most respected art critic in England, was known for discovering and promoting painter J. M. W. Turner (1775–1851; see entry in volume 2), whose swirling atmospheres and hazy light effects recall the very qualities that so disturbed him about Whistler. Whistler reacted to Ruskin's comment by taking the unusual course of suing him for libel—the publication of an untrue statement, in this case, an unfair judgment upon the artistic merit of the work. The trial attracted a great deal of attention for Whistler and for questions of artistic quality that had not normally concerned the general public. Whistler's expensive clothes and witty comments in court contributed to the story, but ultimately the trial turned on the validity of art based on the painter's impressions more than on the actual scene that the painting supposedly captures. In the end, Whistler was victorious, but the jury awarded him only one farthing, a very small amount, and the legal fees forced the artist into bankruptcy. He relocated to Venice in 1880 for a few years and concentrated on etchings, a printing method that he employed to great effect. He also completed several highly regarded portraits of his friends and members of high society.

Interior designs

Whistler's expensive tastes compounded his financial hardship, but in turning to interior design, the artist had reasons beyond recouping his losses. He always believed that for a painting to have the intended effect, the frame had to be exactly right and, furthermore, that every wall, window, rug, and piece of furniture had to work in harmony with the art. It was natural that he would set out to create rooms that fit his lofty ideals.

Masterworks

1858–59	*At the Piano*
1862	*Symphony in White No. 1: The White Girl*
1865–66	*The Artist in His Studio*
1867	*Symphony in White, No. 3*
1871	*Arrangement in Grey and Black: Portrait of the Painter's Mother*
1875	*Nocturne in Black and Gold: The Falling Rocket*
1876–77	*Harmony in Blue and Gold: The Peacock Room*

Japanese design was a major inspiration for Whistler. Whistler's fascination with Japan led him to incorporate Japanese styles into his paintings and to collect Japanese ceramics, but it had its greatest impact in his interior designs. His greatest achievement in this sphere was the *Harmony in Blue and Gold: The Peacock Room* created for the Leyland family's residence at Prince's Gate in London. Created in 1876–77, this project comprises decorative panels, wall treatments, and light fixtures as well as Whistler's own paintings. The entire *Peacock Room* has been reconstructed in the Freer Gallery in Washington, D.C.

In 1888, Whistler married Beatrix Godwin, widow of architect Edward Godwin (1833–1886), but she died eight years later, and Whistler felt the loss deeply. The artist's reputation was at a low point when he died in 1903, but in the decades that followed his achievement was gradually recognized.

For More Information

Books

Adams, Laurie. *Art on Trial: From Whistler to Rothko.* New York: Walker & Co., 1976.

Bendix, Deanna Marohn. *Diabolical Designs: Paintings, Interiors, and Exhibitions of James McNeill Whistler.* Washington, D.C.: Smithsonian Institution Press, 1995.

Berman, Avis. *James McNeill Whistler.* New York: Harry N. Abrams, 1993.

Weintraub, Stanley. *Whistler: A Biography.* New York: Weybright and Talley, 1974.

Whistler, James McNeill. *The Gentle Art of Making Enemies.* Dover, 1991.

Web Sites

"James McNeill Whistler: American Etcher." *Redruth.* [Online] Available http://www.redruth.com (last accessed on July 5, 2001).

"Whistler, James Abbott McNeill." *WebMuseum, Paris.* [Online] Available http://www.ibiblio.org/wm/paint/auth/whistler (last accessed on July 5, 2001).

Grant Wood

Born February 13, 1891
Anamosa, Iowa
Died February 12, 1942
Iowa City, Iowa

American painter and printmaker

"And so, to my great joy, I discovered that in the very commonplace, in my native surroundings, were decorative adventures that my only difficulty had been in taking them too much for granted."

The picture of a farmer, gripping a pitchfork, and a woman standing beside him, is one of the most recognizable images of the twentieth century. Not everybody knows that the painting's title is *American Gothic,* and fewer still know the name of its creator. Grant Wood was an unassuming artist who spent most of his life in the state of Iowa, largely ignoring the artistic trends practiced in nearby Chicago, Illinois, let alone the art capitals of New York City and Paris, France.

Wood sought to capture the ruggedness of his fellow Iowans and the plain rural landscape in which they lived. However, he did not always go about this task in complete seriousness. Rather than a straightforward celebration of the people and the land, his vision takes into account the eccentricities and flaws in the inhabitants of a world he knew so well. This gently satirical perspective, observable in *American Gothic* if one knows to look for it, has endeared Wood all the more to Iowans and anybody who appreciates the spirit of the American Midwest.

Farm drawings

The family of Francis Maryville Wood, the artist's father, were Quakers, a peace-loving Christian sect that flourished in the United States in the nineteenth century. The Woods arrived in eastern Iowa by wagon, and Francis Wood became a farmer. The family of Hattie Weaver, the artist's schoolteacher mother, moved to Iowa from upstate New York in the 1840s.

The second of four children, Grant Wood loved to draw animals around the farm, especially chickens. When he was ten years old, his father died, and the family moved to Cedar Rapids, but farm memories continued to appear in his drawings. At age fourteen, he won an art contest sponsored by a crayon company. In high school, Wood met Marvin Cone, who shared his interest in art, and a lifelong friendship began. For years, the two of them read *The Craftsman* magazine columnist Ernest A. Batchelder (1875–1957) and upon graduation Wood moved to Minneapolis and registered for the School of Design to study under Batchelder. The curriculum was rooted more in craft than fine art, and during this time Wood developed an interest in, and wrote articles on, the building of log cabins.

In 1913, he moved to Chicago, where he took evening courses at the School of the Art Institute and found work in a silversmith's shop. He started a jewelry-making venture with one of his colleagues from the shop, but it never got off the ground. During this time, Chicago hosted "The Armory Show," an important exhibition of avant-garde art from Europe. Avant-garde movements such as impressionism and cubism challenged prevailing ideals about what art could look like, but Wood preferred to stick to traditional and realistic methods. In *The Dutchman's, Old House with Tree Shadows,* (1916) for example, the tree and the house are solid, not atmospheric and dissolved into light, as an impressionist might have rendered them.

Returns to Iowa

In World War I (1914–18), Wood was stationed in Washington, D.C., but poor health prevented him from doing much more than sketching his fellow soldiers. In 1918, the war

◀ Self-portrait of Grant Wood. Courtesy of the Library of Congress.

ended, and he moved back to Cedar Rapids. He took a job teaching art in a junior high school. Despite frequently oversleeping and often forgetting to keep attendance records, Wood was considered an excellent teacher. His favorite activity was enlisting the students' assistance in decorating the school with murals. He continued to work on paintings of local scenes, and in 1919 Killian's Department Store held an exhibition of paintings by Wood and Cone.

Wood also taught high school for awhile. The chief advantage of a teaching job was summer vacation, and in 1920, he and Cone took the first of several trips to Europe together. They traveled to Antwerp, Belgium, where the Olympics were taking place, but instead of attending athletic events, they went to the art museums and studied the works of painters such as Peter Paul Rubens (1577–1640; see entry in volume 2). Despite Rubens's fame for inventing mythological scenes, what attracted Wood most was his eye for detail. They also saw Paris and London, where the crypts of Westminster Abbey fascinated Wood. In the fall of 1923, he took art classes in Paris's Académie Julien and then took an extended vacation in Italy.

A full-time artist

In 1924, a wealthy art lover named David Turner made an offer: Wood and his mother could live on the second floor of a Cedar Rapids mansion Turner sought to convert into a funeral home if the artist decorated it and provided paintings. He used the opportunity to develop some of his European sketches into full-blown paintings, including *Road to Florence* and *Ville d'Avray,* painted at a pond previously immortalized by the French artist Camille Corot (1796–1875). When the 1924–25 school year ended, Wood left teaching behind, and while true success still seemed out of reach, at thirty-three years old he was eager to devote all his time to art.

The paintings in the funeral home appealed to other morticians, and soon many of the Cedar Rapids funeral homes had Grant Wood paintings on their walls. The artist realized that in order to expand his potential audience, he had to cultivate the local arts community. In 1926, he and a singer, Edna Barrett

What Is American Art?

Compared to most other nations the world over, the United States has not had an especially long history, but in its more than two centuries, it has seen a varied array of artistic styles. Part of the reason for this variety is the immigrant experience. The steady arrival of people from all over the world to these shores bolsters what Robert Hughes identifies in his book *American Visions* as "a passionate belief in reinvention and in the American power to make things up as you go along." The most significant musical expression of this tendency is jazz, which depends on players' ability to improvise, or create melodies and rhythms spontaneously. American painters, sculptors, photographers, filmmakers, and so on, have also discovered freedoms in making things up as they go along.

It took a long time for artists in the United States to develop the confidence to do things their own way. Native American cultures had developed a wealth of artistic traditions before the first European immigrants arrived in the seventeenth century. Rather than adopting these traditions, however, the first century or so of American-born artists with European roots that achieved success—including Gilbert Stuart (1755–1828), Thomas Eakins (1844–1916), and **John Singer Sargent** (1856–1925; see entry in volume 4)—relied heavily on the examples of European art. One notable exception to this rule was Edward Hicks (1780–1849), a Quaker preacher whose many versions of a work called *The Peaceable Kingdom* are painted with a childlike simplicity.

In the second half of the twentieth century, American art took off in many directions at once, decisively escaping its European influences. The two most notable art movements of this period, abstract expressionism and pop art, arose in New York City, not coincidentally the most popular first stop of immigrants arriving in America. New York is not the only site of activity, however. From Iowa's Grant Wood to Indiana' Bruce Nauman (1941–), American art is continually revitalized by artists in all fifty states.

Jackson, opened the Fine Arts Studio Group for "Study and Teaching; Interpretation and Inspiration; Cooperation and Mutual Development." This project allowed Wood to thrive in an artistic climate of the sort he had known in Paris, all without leaving Iowa—which was desirable since he had never learned the French language.

Cedar Rapids started building a war memorial in 1927, and Wood was commissioned to design its large stained-glass window. This laborious process involved making detailed sketches, assessing how the central female figure would look from below, and traveling to Munich, Germany, to oversee the window's manufacture. The project, which took nearly three years, profoundly altered the artist's attitude toward his profession. He discovered the simple power of symmetry, that is, the right and left sides of a picture being equal. And both observing the stained glass process and taking the trip to Germany pointed him toward the late gothic and northern Renaissance art that would indirectly lead to his most famous creation.

Paints *American Gothic*

Wood's version of gothic painting was not especially faithful to the work of the gothic artists he admired, such as Hans Memling (c. 1430–1494), but he took from this period of art the presence of everyday objects and the use of pictures to tell stories. In fact, the "gothic" of the painting's title comes from the house behind the couple, which is in the architectural style known as "Carpenter's Gothic."

Wood found the house in the village of Eldon, Iowa, in 1930 and first sketched his sister Nan and his dentist, B. H. McKeeby, on the back of an envelope. In the sketch, McKeeby is holding a rake; by putting a pitchfork in his hand in the final version, Wood hit upon an eerie set of similarities in the shape of the implement, the man's head, and the window behind him. The faces are stern and hard to decipher, and this mystery partially accounts for the picture's enduring appeal. To preserve the mystery, Wood refrained from commenting explicitly on the story behind *American Gothic,* never explaining whether it shows a husband and wife or a father and daughter.

The Art Institute of Chicago purchased the work for three hundred dollars. Commentators were immediately divided over its quality, with some seeing an affectionate portrayal of rural people while others viewed it as insulting. It has gone on to be one of the most parodied pictures in American art, the basis of hundreds of movie posters and magazine covers.

Satire and success

In works produced after *American Gothic,* Wood developed his unique perspective, celebrating the landscape and people of Iowa without getting sentimental over them. *Daughters of Revolution* (1932) shows the artist's capacity for impatience and hostility. The three women in the picture belonged to a group that claimed to have patriotic interests at heart when they objected to the 1927 stained-glass war memorial being produced in Germany, which had been America's enemy during the war, but for Wood the viewpoint they expressed was narrow minded. His portrayal of the *Shriners' Quartet,* a print from 1939, is also satirical, but the "victims" are treated much less harshly; each singer has his own personality.

In 1934, Wood took on two new roles: director of Iowa's Public Works of Art Project and associate professor of fine arts at the University of Iowa. He became a passionate advocate of regionalism, the belief that art and literature produced in small towns, rather than the big cities, reflected the true American spirit. In a speech titled "Revolt against the City," Wood stated, "All I contend for is the sincere use of native material by the artist who has command of it."

Such views were also propounded by Wood's contemporaries, Thomas Hart Benton (1889–1975) and John Steuart Curry (1897–1946). In literature, regionalism was represented by Sinclair Lewis (1885–1951), who in 1930 became the first American to be awarded the prestigious Nobel Prize for Literature, and in 1936 Wood undertook a series of illustrations for Lewis's novel *Main Street* (1920). He created portrayals of personality types such as "The Good Influence" and "The Sentimental Yearner," as well as scenes of the fictional town.

Wood's last great satirical painting, *Parson Weems' Fable* looks at a myth—future president George Washington (1732–1799) confessing to his father that he chopped down a cherry tree—and the mythmaker behind it. Strangely, the young Washington has the head of grown man. This was Wood's way of poking fun at the story, without intending to dishonor the Father of Our Country. The artist died of liver cancer in February of 1942, and *Time* magazine ran an obituary tribute stating, "More than any other painter in the United States he expressed the unabashed simplicity and dignified realism that lay behind the complacent, materialistic exterior of rural Midwestern life." Later the same year, the Art Institute of Chicago held a memorial exhibition of forty-eight works.

Masterworks	
1927–29	*Memorial Window*
1930	*American Gothic*
1932	*Daughters of Revolution*
1939	*Parson Weems' Fable*
	Shriners' Quartet

For More Information

Books

Brown, Hazel E. *Grant Wood and Marvin Cone: Artists of an Era.* Ames: The Iowa State University Press, 1972.

Dennis, James M. *Grant Wood.* Columbia: University of Missouri Press, 1986.

Dennis, James M. *Renegade Regionalists: Grant Wood, Thomas Hart Benton, and John Steuart Curry As Independent Modernists.* Madison: University of Wisconsin Press, 1998.

Web Sites

"American Gothic Parodies." [Online] Available: http://www.bcpl.net/~glake/am.html (last accessed on July 5, 2001).

"Grant Wood." *Cedar Rapids Museum of Art.* [Online] Available: http://www.crma.org/collection/wood/wood.htm (last accessed on July 5, 2001).

"Grant Wood: American Artist" [Online] Available: http://www.ben.esu6.k12.ne.us/ite/wood/ (last accessed on July 5, 2001).

Christopher Wren

Born October 20, 1632
East Knoyle, Wiltshire, England

Died February 25, 1723
London, England

English architect

N o visit to London, England, would be complete without seeing St. Paul's Cathedral, the monumental, beautiful church designed by architect Christopher Wren. While he is known as the finest English architect of the era, Wren also studied mathematics and astronomy, becoming a professor in his mid-twenties. He did not design his first building until he was nearly thirty years old. He made up for lost time, however, designing several of London's finest and most cherished churches, numerous royal palaces, and important structures at Oxford and Cambridge Universities. In the hundreds of years since his death, the appeal of Wren's work has fluctuated with the changing tastes in architectural styles. By the 1920s, however, as stated in Harold Hutchison's biography *Sir Christopher Wren*, his "final position as one of the greatest of architects [could] be regarded as safe and assured."

"Reader, if you seek his monument, look about you."

The inscription on Christopher Wren's tomb, located in St. Paul's Cathedral

▲ *Christopher Wren. Reproduced by permission of Archive Photos.*

A Renaissance man

Born in the county of Wiltshire in southern England, Christopher Wren grew up in a household that had close ties to the royal family. His father was the rector, or religious leader, of the parish church, and when Christopher was a young child, the elder Wren was appointed to an important position in the court of the English king, Charles I (1600–1649). Growing up in such an environment exposed Wren to many of the leading intellectuals in England. Wren developed an interest in mathematics and science, particularly astronomy, as a child.

In 1649, Wren began attending Wadham College at Oxford University, earning a bachelor of arts degree two years later. Living in the later years of the historical era known as the Renaissance, Wren embodied the Renaissance notion that a person should excel in a variety of disciplines. An intellectually curious and vigorous student, he distinguished himself in several scientific fields, studying anatomy and the laws of motion as well as his specialty, astronomy. In 1657, he became a professor of astronomy at Gresham College in London, and four years later he was appointed to the same post at the prestigious Oxford University. Since his student days at Oxford, Wren had been a member of a group of scientists who held meetings to discuss scientific findings. In 1661, having gained the attention and approval of King Charles II (1630–1685), this group became the Royal Society, an organization that still exists and is among the most prestigious scientific societies in the world.

Having grown up amidst royalty in the court of Charles I, Wren understood how to approach a monarch and appreciated the value of his approval. In 1660, Wren sent some drawings he had made of insects under a microscope to King Charles II. Impressed by the young man's talent, the king requested that Wren make a model of the moon. Wren again succeeded in gaining the favor of the king, who became convinced that Wren could accomplish anything, regardless of whether he had been formally trained in a certain field. Although Wren had never been trained as an architect, Charles II asked him to design some modifications to an English naval base located in

Tangier, a city in Morocco. While Wren respectfully declined that offer, he knew that the king's confidence in him would prove extremely helpful in his career.

It turned out that the king's trust in Wren was not misplaced. Wren's education and research—particularly his knowledge of physics and geometry—proved invaluable for a career in architecture, a field that blends science, mathematics, and art in equal measure. In 1662, Wren was hired to design his first building: the Sheldonian Theatre, a gift to Oxford University by a London bishop named Gilbert Sheldon (1598–1677). The Sheldonian, a large hall designed for use in official university ceremonies and meetings, reflects Wren's creative touch and his ability to resolve structural problems in an innovative manner. He developed a system of beams, hidden above the ceiling, to support the seventy-foot-wide roof. These beams, called a truss, meant that the roof did not need to be supported by pillars, which would have blocked the view of spectators in the building.

The Great Fire of London

While architecture in much of Western Europe experienced a creative explosion during the Renaissance period, England lagged behind. Architecture in France and Italy had benefited from the Renaissance emphasis on reviving the classical styles of ancient Greece and Rome. England, on the other hand, because of its geographical distance from and political conflicts with Western European nations, had not absorbed the classical influence so prominent in other countries. In an effort to learn from the exciting developments taking place on the continent, Wren traveled to Paris, France, in 1665. There he met with the country's most famous architects, viewing their drawings and their buildings under construction. Deeply impressed by the Louvre Palace, the Palace of Versailles, and some of the great domed churches of Paris, Wren returned to England in 1666 full of ideas and inspiration. Later that year, an unfortunate circumstance led to an opportunity for Wren to put those ideas into practice.

On September 2, 1666, a fire broke out in the center of London, an area known as the City. The fire raged for four days, destroying or damaging a number of government buildings, thousands of houses, and dozens of churches, including the old St. Paul's Cathedral. The Great Fire reduced the City to ashes, but for Wren the destruction translated into a need for rebuilding. He promptly submitted a plan for a redesign of the London streets, and while that plan was never implemented, Wren eventually became instrumental to the City's reconstruction. He was appointed a member of the commission that would oversee reconstruction, and in 1669 Charles II named Wren surveyor-general of the Royal Works, which meant that Wren was the country's chief architect and would oversee all royal building projects. In that same year, Wren married Faith Coghill; they had two sons together before her death in 1675; their first son, Gilbert, died when just a baby, but their second son, Christopher, lived to the age of seventy-two.

St. Paul's Cathedral

Wren held the post of surveyor-general until 1718, and during the intervening years he designed or consulted on more than fifty churches, working as well on several royal palaces and hospitals. While many of his buildings reveal his exceptional skill, St. Paul's Cathedral is undoubtedly his masterpiece. But the church's magnificence did not come easily: more than forty years passed from when Wren first began his design in 1669 until construction was completed in 1710. Wren's design for the new cathedral had to please several parties with varying tastes and interests, including King Charles II, England's religious leaders, and London's prominent business owners. His first design, completed in 1670, was considered too small and modest—many people felt that St. Paul's should have more grandeur, befitting a great capital city like London. For the second design, Wren took his cue from the classically influenced architecture seen on the European continent. He planned for the church to take the basic shape of a Greek cross, that is, a cross with all arms being equal in size. This shape mirrored that of St. Peter's Basilica in Rome, Italy

—a world-famous church that represents the heart of the Catholic religion. The king loved this design, urging Wren to make a wooden model of the cathedral. This highly detailed structure, measuring twenty feet long and known as the Great Model, still exists and can be seen on display in the Trophy Room at St. Paul's. The English clergy strongly opposed this design, primarily because they objected to its similarity to the famous Catholic church. The Protestant Church of England, having only separated from the Catholic Church about 130 years earlier, felt anxious to establish its independence in every way possible. To his great disappointment, and in spite of the king's approval, Wren was eventually persuaded to abandon his Great Model.

The final design, called the Warrant design because it received the king's royal warrant, or authorization, clearly

St. Paul's Cathedral (1675–1708). Designed by Christopher Wren. Photograph, © Adam Woolfitt. Reproduced by permission of the Corbis Corporation.

shows compromises on Wren's part. A combination of several different styles, the Warrant design is basically a Gothic-style church with some classical decoration. England's Gothic churches (referring to a style popular between the twelfth and the sixteenth centuries), built to cover a large area rather than extend to great heights, represented a proud historical tradition, and England's religious leaders wished for St. Paul's to continue in that tradition. The Warrant design was approved in 1675. As it happened, however, Wren departed significantly from this plan, making numerous changes as construction progressed, and the actual cathedral bears little resemblance to the design on which it was supposedly based.

Construction of St. Paul's began in 1675. Wren imported stone from all over England and from northern France, and he hired the finest carpenters and masons, or stoneworkers. The first service in the new cathedral was held in 1697, though the dome had not yet been built and the building was far from finished. Thirty-five years after construction began, in 1710, the cathedral was finally completed. Wren was seventy-nine years old. His masterwork is an impressive, dramatic building topped by a magnificent dome that still, after hundreds of years, holds a prominent place in the London skyline. To decorate the interior, Wren hired extremely skillful craftspeople and artists. Their intricate work in iron, wood, and stone complements the grandeur of Wren's structure. While architectural experts have noted that Wren's design suffers somewhat from the compromises he made, St. Paul's is considered to be one of the world's finest churches. Millions of people from all over the world visit the cathedral each year—it is one of the most popular tourist destinations in all of London.

Beyond St. Paul's

A man of tremendous energy and creativity, Wren did not content himself with working solely on St. Paul's Cathedral during the decades it took to build it. Throughout those years, he experienced many hardships and joys in his personal life. In 1677, two years after his first wife's death, Wren married Jane Fitzwilliam, and the couple had two children, a daughter

◀ *Mosaicwork of the ceiling of the choir in St. Paul's Cathedral (1675–1710). Designed by Christopher Wren.* Photograph, © Angelo Hornak. Reproduced by permission of the Corbis Corporation.

Masterworks

1670–80	St. Mary-le-Bow (church)
1672–79	St. Stephen, Walbrook
1675–1710	St. Paul's Cathedral
1676–84	Trinity College Library
1681–82	Tom's Tower
1681–86	St. Mary Abchurch
1682–91	Royal Hospital at Chelsea
1689–1702	Hampton Court Palace
1696–1702	Greenwich Hospital

named Jane and a son named William. Unfortunately, his second wife lived only until 1679, Wren's beloved daughter died in her twenties, and his son William was born with a severe mental handicap.

Wren's professional life perhaps served as a distraction from personal sorrows. In addition to overseeing the building of St. Paul's and dozens of other glorious churches, Wren was also the architect of the library at Cambridge University's Trinity College and the main gateway, called Tom's Tower, of Christ Church College at Oxford University. He made massive renovations to several royal palaces in England as well as building the Royal Hospital at Chelsea (near London) and the Greenwich Hospital (later the Royal Naval College), which was completed after his death. Wren dominated architecture in England for more than fifty years, and while many of his buildings have since been destroyed, his legacy can still be seen throughout London and surrounding areas. The great architect died in his London home at the age of ninety. He was buried in the crypt at St. Paul's.

For More Information

Books

Chambers, James. *Christopher Wren.* Stroud, England: Sutton Publishing, 1998.

Hutchison, Harold. *Sir Christopher Wren.* New York: Stein and Day, 1976.

Whinney, Margaret. *Wren.* London: Thames & Hudson, 1998.

Web Sites

St. Paul's Cathedral Online. [Online] Available http://www.stpauls.co.uk/rindex.htm (last accessed on July 5, 2001).

"Sir Christopher Wren." *Great Buildings Collection.* [Online] Available http://www.greatbuildings.com/architects/Sir_Christopher_Wren.html (last accessed on July 5, 2001).

University of St. Andrews, Scotland. "Sir Christopher Wren." *The MacTutor History of Mathematics Archive.* [Online] Available http://www-history.mcs.st-andrews.ac.uk/history/Mathematicians/Wren.html (last accessed on July 5, 2001).

Andrew Wyeth

Born July 12, 1917
Chadds Ford, Pennsylvania

American painter

"In the art world today, I'm so conservative I'm radical. Most painters don't care for me. I'm strange to them."

▲ *Andrew Wyeth.*
Photograph, © Richard Schulman. Reproduced by permission of the Corbis Corporation.

One of the most popular American painters of all time, Andrew Wyeth is best known for realistically painted landscapes of the rural eastern United States. While his traditional style and limited range of subjects has not won him many fans among the more experimental and adventurous in the art community, it has earned him millions of admirers among the general public. Wyeth's barren, windswept landscapes, depicting the two communities in Pennsylvania and Maine in which he has spent his entire life, convey loneliness and sadness as well as a love for the regions' subtle beauty. In addition to landscapes, Wyeth has also painted people, doing numerous portraits of friends, neighbors, and family in a style that is nearly photographic in its realism. The son of painter and illustrator N. C. Wyeth (1882–1945), Andrew Wyeth has, after a career of more than sixty years, established himself as an artist with a singular connection to the American countryside.

Growing up in Chadds Ford and Maine

In 1907, ten years before Andrew Wyeth's birth, his parents, N. C. and Carolyn Wyeth, moved to Chadds Ford, Pennsylvania, a farming community in the Brandywine River Valley where Wyeth still lives. Andrew was the youngest of five children born into a family that cherished art, music, and imagination as well as the countryside where they lived. N. C. Wyeth was a successful commercial artist and illustrator who is perhaps best remembered for his illustrations of such childhood literary classics as *Treasure Island, Kidnapped,* and *Robin Hood.* N. C. Wyeth also had aspirations as a fine artist, though he had difficulty gaining acceptance in that field due to his commercial work. Taking an active, dominant role in his children's lives, he schooled his elder daughters in the basics of drawing and painting when they were very young. A sensitive and frequently ill child, Andrew was kept out of school and tutored at home. When he was fifteen, he began his formal artistic training, joining the classes his father taught to beginning art students.

Early in his artistic training, Andrew Wyeth decided that watercolors were his preferred medium. And, after a childhood with long hours spent exploring the countryside near his home, he found himself drawn to capturing landscapes in his paintings. At the age of sixteen, Wyeth saw some paintings of American watercolorist Winslow Homer (1836–1910) and Homer's exceptional use of light and tone made a deep impression on the young man. From his father, Wyeth learned precision in drawing, a skill he would not fully explore until years later. His early works were impressionistic watercolors, capturing with bold colors and quick, imprecise brush strokes the feelings conjured up by a particular scene. He painted scenes around his home in Chadds Ford as well as the area where the Wyeth family spent their summers in Maine. These two locales would play a dominant role throughout Wyeth's career.

In 1936, Wyeth participated in his first exhibit, in Philadelphia, Pennsylvania. The following year marked his first solo exhibit, a show at the Macbeth Gallery in New York City. At twenty years old, Wyeth had begun to establish himself as a fine artist. His works at the Macbeth show sold out in two days. Two years later, in 1939, Wyeth met Betsy Merle James in Maine. An attractive and dynamic woman, James immediately captured Wyeth's attention, and the two were married the following spring. They later went on to have two sons, Nicholas, born in 1943, and Jamie, born in 1946. Jamie grew up to continue the family tradition, becoming an artist in his own right.

A new direction

By the early 1940s, Wyeth had begun to alter his style. No longer satisfied with his impressionist-style watercolors, Wyeth began to paint using egg tempera, a combination of egg yolk and pigment. He felt that tempera gave his works a depth that the watercolors lacked, and the fact that tempera dries quickly forced him to paint with greater accuracy and speed. He continued to paint in watercolor occasionally, using a technique called drybrush. With drybrush, almost all of the liquid is squeezed out of the paintbrush, resulting in a very fine, precise line like that of a pencil. Both drybrush and tempera allowed Wyeth to capture with impressive accuracy the cracks in a stone wall, the veins in a leaf, and the wrinkles on a face.

Wyeth's life was marked by tragedy in October 1945 when his father and three-year-old nephew were killed after their car stalled in the path of an oncoming train. The death of N. C. Wyeth, who had been such a powerful force in Wyeth's life, left the painter both deeply grieved and determined to make a change in his life. He felt that, up until then, he had not pursued his art seriously enough, and he resolved that his skills and training would not be wasted. A few months after his father's death, Wyeth began a painting that signaled his new direction as a painter; it also reflected his grief for the loss of his father. While visiting the railroad crossing where the accident took place, Wyeth saw a boy running quickly and clumsily down a nearby hill. In Wyeth's mind, the slope of the land represented his father, while the boy represented Wyeth, running perhaps to release his sorrow but also to express his freedom from his father's expectations. In the painting, called

Winter 1946, one of the boy's hands drifts away from his body in a gesture of release, and Wyeth has commented that "that hand drifting in the air was my free soul, groping." *Winter 1946,* with its muted earth tones, realistic rendering of the landscape, and lonely, bleak mood, marked the crystallization of a style that Wyeth would pursue for decades to come.

Wyeth remarked that after his father's death, he "saw the country even more simplified and somber, saw what the whole country meant." The countryside, and the people that populated it, continued to provide inspiration for Wyeth throughout his career, both in Chadds Ford and in Maine. In 1939, Wyeth's wife Betsy had introduced him to her friends Christina and Alvaro Olson, a brother and sister who lived in an eighteenth-century farmhouse near Cushing, Maine. Captivated by the beauty of their property as well as the Olsons themselves, Wyeth has featured the Olson home in many of his paintings, including *Weather Side* and *Wind from the Sea.* Christina, paralyzed since her youth but still displaying a strong spirit and

Winter, 1946 (1946). Painting by Andrew Wyeth. Tempera on board. 31⅜ x 48 in (79.7 x 121.9 cm) © North Carolina Museum of Art. Photograph reproduced by permission of the Corbis Corporation.

generous personality, represented many qualities that Wyeth admired. In 1948, Wyeth painted what is perhaps his most famous work: *Christina's World.* This painting shows Christina—her pink dress standing out against the muted browns and greys of the landscape—dragging herself across a field toward her house. Wyeth's skillful use of perspective, with Christina dominating the foreground and her house on a hill in the distance, gives the painting a dramatic quality that has appealed to audiences for generations. The picture was acquired by the Museum of Modern Art in New York, where it remains one of its most popular works.

Another family whose members and home became important to Wyeth were the Kuerners, a German couple who lived on a farm near the Wyeths' house in Chadds Ford. Many biographers have suggested that Karl Kuerner became a father figure for Wyeth after the 1945 accident. Wyeth admired Kuerner's strength and his self-sufficient lifestyle. The contrast between the beauty of the land where he lived and the brutality of Kuerner's hunting and slaughtering of animals sparked Wyeth's imagination, and over the years he painted scenes of life on the Kuerner farm many times. Some of the more notable paintings of the property include *Groundhog Day* and *Brown Swiss,* but it was a portrait of Karl that became one of Wyeth's most important works. Painted in 1948, *Karl* is painted as though the artist were looking up at Kuerner's face. That perspective, as well as the dramatic lighting that leaves part of Kuerner's face in shadow, results in a powerful, disturbing portrait. The impact of the image is heightened by the presence of sharp hooks, used for hanging sausages, embedded in the cracked ceiling over Kuerner's head.

The Helga pictures

Wyeth's relationship to the Kuerners later led to his most well known subject: Helga Testorf. Wyeth came into contact with Helga, a German immigrant, when she began working for the Kuerner family. In the early 1970s, he began drawing and painting Helga without telling anyone, including his wife, and he continued doing so for nearly fifteen years. In 1986, Wyeth

Refuge, *one of the hundreds of paintings from Andrew Wyeth's "Helga" collection (1970–1985).* Photograph, © Geoffrey Clements. Reproduced by permission of the Corbis Corporation.

revealed the collection to his wife, and then to the world. The works, about 240 in all, caused a major stir in the artistic community and among the general public. Wyeth was a very well known artist at the time, and the unveiling of a collection of that size, all devoted to a single model, was newsworthy. One of the Helga paintings, called *Braids,* made the cover of both *Time* and *Newsweek* magazines. Most of the Helga pictures were bought by a collector, Leonard E. B. Andrews, who considered them a "national treasure" and proceeded to call as much attention to them as possible. Receiving extraordinary publicity, the entire collection was first displayed at the National Gallery of Art in Washington, D.C., and then traveled to other major American cities. While millions of people flocked to the exhibit and many critics praised Wyeth's newly revealed works, others were suspicious of the media hype and critical of Wyeth's commercialism. Some even speculated that the Wyeths had deliberately kept the collection a secret to create a stir and raise the value of the Helga pictures.

The works themselves, including pencil drawings and watercolor, tempera, and drybrush paintings, depict Helga indoors and out, clothed and nude, walking through the woods and sleeping on a bed. With his characteristic detail and precision, Wyeth captured Helga in an intimate way, prompting much speculation about the nature of their relationship. Some critics found the collection a bit repetitious, while others commented that many of the works, particularly the nudes, reveal an artist at the height of his powers. The critical disagreements surrounding the Helga pictures were just one chapter in a long-running dispute among art lovers over the quality of Wyeth's art. Many have considered Wyeth's works too sentimental and melodramatic, suggesting that they fail to challenge viewers, either visually or intellectually. In a reference to Wyeth's father's career as a commercial artist, some critics have dismissed Wyeth as an illustrator rather than a fine artist.

On the other hand, Wyeth has earned the admiration of millions of fans as well as the approval of many established institutions. Wyeth's works have been exhibited at several prestigious museums, with a 1967 retrospective exhibit breaking attendance records at the Whitney Museum of American Art in New York. His painting *Her Room,* bought by the Farnsworth Art Museum in Rockland, Maine, fetched the highest price ever paid by a museum for the work of a living artist. Wyeth was awarded the Medal of Freedom by President John F. Kennedy (1917–1963) in 1963, and he became the first American artist since **John Singer Sargent** (1856–1925; see entry in volume 4) to be accepted into the distinguished Académie des Beaux-Arts (Academy of Fine Arts) in France. Some have explained the critical disapproval as the expected reaction to an old-fashioned artist working during a period of great experimentation. Much twentieth-century art is devoted to exploring progressive and unconventional means of expression, and in such an era, a traditional artist like Wyeth is an oddity who is bound to attract negative attention.

For More Information

Books and Periodicals

Gardner, John. "But Is It Good?" *National Review* 50 (August 3, 1998): p. 54.

The Helga Pictures. New York: Harry N. Abrams, Inc., 1987.

Meryman, Richard. *Andrew Wyeth* (First Impressions series). New York: Harry N. Abrams, Inc., 1991.

Updike, John. "Heavily Hyped Helga: The Artist and the Girl Next Door." *The New Republic* 197 (December 7, 1987): p. 27.

Venn, Beth, et al. *Unknown Terrain: The Landscapes of Andrew Wyeth.* New York: Whitney Museum of American Art, 1998.

Wyeth, Andrew. *Andrew Wyeth: Autobiography.* Boston: Bullfinch Press, 1995.

Web Sites

"Andrew Wyeth." *Mark Harden's Artchive.* [Online] Available http://www.artchive.com/artchive/W/wyeth.html (last accessed on July 5, 2001).

"Unknown Terrain: The Landscapes of Andrew Wyeth." *Traditional Fine Art Online.* [Online] Available http://www.tfaoi.com/newsml/n1m153.htm (last accessed on July 5, 2001).

The Wyeth Center. [Online] Available http://www.wyethcenter.com/ (last accessed on June 8, 2001).

Further Reading

Laurie Anderson

The following list focuses on works written for readers of middle school or high school age. Books aimed at adult readers have been included when they are especially important in providing information or analysis that would otherwise be unavailable, or because they have become classics.

Books

Adams, Laurie Schneider. *A History of Western Art.* New York: Harry N. Abrams, Inc., 1994.

Adams, Steven. *The Impressionists.* Philadelphia: Running Press, 1990.

Atkins, Robert. *Artspeak: A Guide to Contemporary Ideas, Movements, and Buzzwords, 1945 to the Present.* New York: Abbeville, 1990.

Atkins, Robert. *Artspoke: A Guide to Modern Ideas, Movements, and Buzzwords, 1848-1944.* New York: Abbeville, 1993.

Encyclopedia of Artists. 6 vols. New York: Oxford University Press, 2000.

Encyclopedia of World Biography, 2nd ed. 17 vols. Detroit: Gale, 1998.

George Eastman House. *Photography from 1839 to Today.* Cologne, Germany: Taschen, 2000.

Gombrich, E. H. *The Story of Art.* London: Phaidon Press Limited, 1995.

The Grove Dictionary of Art. 34 vols. New York: Macmillan, 1996.

Harris, Ann Sutherland, and Linda Nochlin. *Women Artists, 1550–1950.* New York: Knopf, 1976.

Held, Julius S., and Donald Posner. *17th and 18th Century Art.* New York: Prentice Hall and Harry N. Abrams, Inc., 1972.

Heller, Jules, and Nancy G. Heller. *North American Women Artists of the Twentieth Century.* New York: Garland Publishing, 1995.

Janson, H. W., and Anthony F. Janson. *History of Art for Young People.* New York: Harry N. Abrams, Inc., 1997.

Labella, Vincenzo. *A Season of Giants, 1492—1508: Michelangelo, Leonardo, Raphael.* Boston: Little, Brown and Company, 1990.

Lucie-Smith, Edward. *Visual Arts in the Twentieth Century.* New York: Harry N. Abrams, Inc., 1996.

Lynton, Norbert. *A History of Art: An Introduction to Painting and Sculpture.* New York: Warwick Press, 1981.

Merlo, Claudio. *The History of Art: From Ancient to Modern Times.* Chicago: Peter Bedrick Books, 2000.

Ridley, Pauline. *Modern Art.* New York: Thomson Learning, 1995.

Rosenblum, Robert, and H. W. Janson. *19th-Century Art.* New York: Harry N. Abrams, Inc., 1984.

Tansey, Richard G., and Fred S. Kleiner. *Gardner's Art through the Ages.* Fort Worth, TX: Harcourt Brace College Publishers, 1996.

Toman, Rolf, ed. *The Art of the Italian Renaissance: Architecture, Sculpture, Painting, Drawing.* San Diego, CA: Thunder Bay Press, 1995.

Walther, Ingo F., ed. *Art of the 20th Century.* 2 vols. Cologne, Germany: Taschen, 1998.

Web sites

About Art History. [Online] Available http://arthistory.about.com/arts/arthistory/ (accessed May 23, 2001).

All About Artists. [Online] Available http://allaboutartists.com/ (accessed May 23, 2001).

Art History Resources on the Web. [Online] Available http:// witcombe.sbc.edu/ARTHLinks.html (accessed May 23, 2001).

Artcyclopedia. [Online] Available http://www.artcyclopedia.com/ (accessed May 23, 2001).

Artlex Art Dictionary. [Online] Available http://artlex.com/ (accessed May 23, 2001).

Artnet.com. [Online] Available http://www.artnet.com/library/ (accessed May 23, 2001).

CGFA. [Online] Available http://sunsite.dk/cgfa/ (accessed May 23, 2001).

Great Buildings Online. [Online] Available http://www.greatbuildings.com/ (accessed May 23, 2001).

Mark Harden's Artchive. [Online] Available http://www.artchive.com (accessed May 23, 2001).

Masters of Photography. [Online] Available http://www.masters-of-photography.com (accessed May 23, 2001).

NGA Kids. [Online] Available http://www.nga.gov/kids/ (accessed May 23, 2001).

Web Gallery of Art. [Online] Available http://gallery.euroweb.hu/index.html (accessed May 23, 2001).

WebMuseum, Paris. [Online] Available http://www.ibiblio.org/wm/ (accessed May 23, 2001).

World Wide Arts Resources. [Online] Available http://www.wwar.com (accessed May 23, 2001).

Index

Bold numerals indicate volume numbers; illustrations are marked by (ill.).

Maya Lin

E

Eakins, Thomas, **2:** 425; **4:** 429
Eames, Charles, **4:** 363
Easter and the Totem (Pollock),
  2: 355-356
Easter Monday (de Kooning),
  3: 201
Eastern United States, **4:** 444
East of Borneo (Melford), **77**
Echoes of Harlem (Ringgold),
  4: 317
Edge of Town (Schiele), **4:** 382
Edo period, 1603-1868 (Japan),
  3: 152-153, 158
Edward MacDowell Medal,
  4: 263-264
Edwards, John, **3:** 18, 19
Edward Weston (Springer),
  4: 239
"Eggbeater Series" (Davis), **1:** 98
Egypt, **3:** 186
The Eiffel Tower (Seurat), **2:** 415
El Espolio (*The Disrobing of
  Christ;* El Greco), **1:** 162
El Greco, 1: 119, **158-165;**
  2: 436
Eliot, T. S., **3:** 17
El Jaleo (Sargent), **4:** 371
El Machete, **4:** 240
Eluard, Gala, **1:** 94
Eluard, Paul, **4:** 221
Eminent Victorians (Wilson),
  3: 50, 54
Empty Places (Anderson), **3:** 6
The Endless Column (Brancusi),
  1: 27
*The Enemy Would Have Been
  Warned ... That My Ship Was
  Below Them* (Lichtenstein),
  2: 261 (ill.)
Engravings, **1:** 113, 115-116
Environmental art, **1:** 82-88
Equation for Jim Beckwourth
  (Puryear), **4:** 290
"Equivalents" series (Stieglitz),
  2: 422
Erasmus, **1:** 119
Ergonomics, **1:** 170
Ernst, Max, **2:** 287; **3:** 74

Escher, M. C., 3: 109-116
Escorial, **1:** 161-162; **2:** 433
Etants Donées. see Given
Etchings, **1:** 152, 154-157, 193
Euclid, **4:** 300
Europe, a Prophecy (Blake), **3:**29
Evergood, Philip, **2:** 385
Everson Art Museum (Syracuse,
  New York), **4:** 257 (ill.)
Excavation (de Kooning), **3:** 198
Existentialism, **4:** 253
Experimental art, **4:** 252-253. *see
  also* Avant-garde
Expressionism, **1:** 149; **4:** 246-247,
  377-378, 380-381. *see also*
  Abstract expressionism

F

F. A. O. Schwarz, **4:** 386-387
The Factory, **2:** 461-465
Faerna, José Marèa, **3:** 182
Fagus-Werk, **1:** 167
Faith Ringgold (Love), **4:** 316 (ill.)
Fallingwater, the Kaufmann
  House (Bear Run, Pennsylvania;
  Wright), **2:** 471-472, 471 (ill.)
Fall (Johns), **3:** 179-180
Fall of the Cowboy (Remington),
  4: 312
False Start (Johns), **3:** 177
Family (Bearden), **1:** 21 (ill.)
The Family of Charles IV (Goya),
  1: 153-**154** (ill.)
Family of Newsvendors, Mexico
  City (Cartier-Bresson), **1:** 45 (ill.)
"Famous Places in Edo: A
  Hundred Views" (Hiroshige),
  3: 157
"Famous Places of the Eastern
  Capital" (Hiroshige), **3:** 156
Fantin-Latour, Henri, **2:** 277
The Farm (Miró), **4:** 229
Farnsworth Art Museum
  (Rockland, Maine), **4:** 450
Fashion photography, **4:** 398-399
Fauvism, **1:** 205-206; **2:** 290, 292,
  294, 305; **3:** 39-40; **4:** 225
Favrile, **4:** 405
Fax machines, art and, **3:** 161-162

G

Milles, Carl, **1:** 175

Milton, John, **3:** 24, 29-30

Minimalism, **4:** 286, 288, 289

Ministry of Public Education
  (Mexico City), **2:** 381

The Miracle of the Spring
  (Giotto), **3:** 134

Miró, Joan, 1: 92; **4: 227-234**

Misery (Modotti), **4:** 241

Mishima, Yukio, **4:** 253

Miss Chicago (Miró), **4:** 233

Mister Heartbreak (Anderson),
  3: 4, 6

MIT. *see* Massachusetts Institute
  of Technology (MIT)

Mitchell, Joan, **1:** 124

Mme. Inès Moitessier Seated
  (Ingres), **3:** 171

Mobiles, **1:** 34, 37-38

Moby Dick (Melville), **3:** 8

Mock, Freida Lee, **3:** 215

Model, Lisette, **3:** 11

Modern architecture, **4:** 364-365,
  366, 367-368

Modern Head (Lichtenstein),
  3: 211 (ill.)

Modigliani, Amedeo, **1:** 28;
  2: 380

Modotti, Tina, 4: 235-243

Moholy-Nagy, Laszlo, **1:** 38,
  170-171

Moilliet, Louis, **3:** 184

Mojotech (Saar), **4:** 358

Mona Lisa (Duchamp), **3:** 178

Mona Lisa (Leonardo). *see La
  Gioconda* (Leonardo)

Mondriaan, Pieter. *see*
  Mondrian, Piet

Mondrian, Piet, 1: 37, 100;
  2: 304-309

Monet, Claude, 2: 310-317
  Braque and, **3:** 39
  Cassatt and, **1:** 50
  Cézanne and, **1:** 59-60
  copies by Lichtenstein,
    2: 263; **3:** 212
  influence on Gauguin, **1:** 138
  influence on Kandinsky,
    1: 205
  influence on Picasso, **2:** 343

influence on Seurat, **2:** 412
influence on van Gogh, **1:** 148
Japanese art and, **3:** 151, 157
Manet and, **2:** 277-278
Munch and, **4:** 245-246
Pissarro and, **4:** 268, 269-270
Renoir and, **2:** 364-366
Sargent and, **4:** 370

Monk, Meredith, **3:** 5; **4:** 255

*Monolith—Moon and Half Dome,
  Yosemite National Park,
  California, 1960* (Adams),
  1: 11 (ill.)

Montagu, Mary Wortley, **3:** 171

Montefeltro, Federigo da, **4:** 295

Montgomery, Alabama,
  2: 268-269

Mont Sainte-Victoire (Cézanne),
  1: 61 (ill.)

Monument for Tirgui Jui
  (Brancusi), **1:** 27

*Monument to the Third
  International* (Tatlin), **4:** 332

*Moonrise, Hernandez, New
  Mexico, 1921* (Adams),
  1: 13 (ill.)

The Moon-Woman (Pollock),
  2: 353

Moore, Demi, **2:** 247

Moore, Henry, 2: 318-323

Moore, Noel, **4:** 282, 283

Morisot, Berthe, **1:** 53; **2:** 278,
  314, 366

Morris, Cedric, **3:** 126-127

Morris, Robert, **4:** 288

Morris, William, **4:** 404

Mosaics, **1:** 160-161

Moscow, Russia, **1:** 69, 204-205

Moses, Anna Mary Robertson,
  4: 350

Mother and Child, Tehuantepec
  (Modotti), **4:** 240

Mother and Infant (Cassatt),
  1: 52 (ill.)

Mother's Day Out (Rockwell),
  4: 324

Motherwell, Robert, **1:** 127;
  4: 233

Motif from Hammamet (Klee),
  3: 184-185